Diversity of Play

The chapters of this book are based on keynote lectures held at DiGRA2015 in Lüneburg. We acknowledge the friendly support of DiGRA (Digital Games Research Association) and its board.

Diversity of Play

edited by
Mathias Fuchs

**Bibliographical Information of the
German National Library**
The German National Library lists this publication in the
Deutsche Nationalbibliografie (German National Biblio-
graphy); detailed bibliographic information is available
online at http://dnb.d-nb.de.

Published in 2015 by meson press, Hybrid Publishing Lab,
Centre for Digital Cultures, Leuphana University of Lüneburg
www.meson-press.com

Design concept: Torsten Köchlin, Silke Krieg
Cover design: Laleh Torabi
Copy-editing: Andrew Stapleton

The print edition of this book is printed by Lightning Source,
Milton Keynes, United Kingdom.

ISBN (Print):   978-3-95796-075-7
ISBN (PDF):   978-3-95796-076-4
ISBN (EPUB):   978-3-95796-077-1
DOI: 10.14619/012

The digital editions of this publication can be downloaded
freely at: www.meson-press.com.

Funded by the EU major project Innovation Incubator
Lüneburg

Contents

Total Gamification: Introduction   7
Mathias Fuchs

Gamification of Gothic   21
Tanya Krzywinska

Video Games as Unnatural Narratives   41
Astrid Ensslin

Is Hacking the Brain the Future of Gaming?   73
Karen Palmer

Navigating Uncertainty: Ludic Epistemology in an Age of New Essentialisms   83
Markus Rautzenberg

Authors   109

Total Gamification

Mathias Fuchs

When a former US vice president calls games "normal", it is most likely that the medium he is talking about has lost its innocence. Al Gore's statement that "games are the new normal" (2011) indicates that the early days when games were new and nice, harmless, or neat and niche, are gone. Games have had their coming of age and the days of ludic infancy are long since past. Through the maturation of games as a medium, we have realised they can serve a purpose and have lost their naïveté. Games can simulate battlefields, games can predict disaster, they can increase profit, and they can crunch markets. On their way to maturity games have lost their enchanting non-intentionality. The original naïveté of being good for nothing but play has vanished into thin air. It has, however, been replaced by a second order naïveté: the interests of games are no longer challenged.[1] Nobody would call a game "corrupted" (Caillois 1958) if money was involved in the gameplay. There are also no taboo areas for gaming. Gaming scenarios include warfare, pornography, financial transactions, espionage and counter-espionage, theft and antisocial behaviour. Welcome to the days of total gamification!

What we experience today is a diversity of play and the ubiquity of games, making them not only a popular medium but also a key medium and probably *the* leading medium of contemporary society.

The coverage of games across media sectors and social niches also makes them a super-medium, a medium that can easily adopt the styles and modes of predecessor media. Games can cannibalise sister media and pretend to be film, radio, narration,

---

1   I pick up an idea here that Adorno formulated in regard to art and its lost "naïveté" (Adorno 2004, 3).

performance or sculpture. Games can adopt genres, or masquerade as medieval, futuristic, elegant, brutal or Gothic. In this book Tanya Krzywinska casts a critical glance upon the pleasure that Gothic forms invoke, and investigates the horror games subculture, a segment that amounts to 20 percent of digital games. Markus Rautzenberg (this volume) describes video games as "an explorable universal metaphor of the digital medium" and points out that we "look through" games to see content without realising that it is the medium we are looking at while at the same time we acknowledge an indispensable distance from the medium. On one hand we can explore simulated worlds without being distracted by pixelation or other display peculiarities, but on the other hand an "uncertainty" still remains about whether we are inside the medium or outside (Rautzenberg, this volume). Our contemporary perception differs from how we experienced games in the days of eight-bit computing: a pixelated view guaranteed a permanent distance from the medium. It can be demonstrated in many instances that distance from a medium accompanies the reception of that medium in its early stages. Irony, laughter and mockery are fuelled by the artefacts, the glitches and the distortions that media, in their infancy, initially produce in abundance. This was the case for the car with its "horse-carriageness", for early radio with its crackle and hiss, and for television with the constraint of 625 horizontal scan lines and half-images.[2] Mature media lose their obvious mediality. Games have grown up and today we consider them "normal" in a way that is not unlike the "normality" of television in the 1960s and '70s.

Astrid Ensslin (2015) looks at the ubiquity and normality of games when she states that she is:

> Not sure whether you can say that (print!) literature was ever as popular and all-pervasive as games are nowadays. Of course there's still the digital divide, but even before

---

2   This is the case for most PAL television format variants.

radio, television and film came to be mass media, literature never had the kind of "mass effect" and the kind of creative, user-driven popular culture that games have today – due to low literacy levels and social discrimination in centuries past. Perhaps you could say that games (and particularly mobile games) are the new television. (Ensslin 2015)

Very much like television was a *conditio sine qua non* in the '50s, games are a must-have now. Today's grandparents have to possess skills in *Angry Birds* (2009) to demonstrate they are cool – and schoolchildren have to be able to cope with gamified learning apps to prove they are clever. Firefighters need serious games to learn how to extinguish fires and the terminally ill have to keep playing to stay in shape. There is hardly a social group or a niche within a population that can do without games. Maybe the insane. But then this only proves what Al Gore told us. If "games are the new normal", then only those who are not normal will not play them.

Seriousness as a Problem

When games started to be considered as being "serious" at least one of two essential sources of resistance[3] against the false notion of a whole, all-encompassing, eco-sociological system became apparent: Games could no longer claim a "resistant" distance to empirical reality. Serious games, on the contrary, increasingly mingled with empirical reality and with the "regime of representation" in a way that was unprecedented. For years, children have been playing doctors and nurses or soldiers and police, but never before have games been declared medically effective or been applied to organise battlefield operations. The success of gamification and serious games established a deep belief in the paradoxical notion of serious play and the equally

3   Rancière speaks of the regime of representation and of the aesthetic regime
     (Rancière 2008, 15–17).

surprising concept of games in "non-gaming contexts". The evangelists of gamification proclaimed that everybody could live longer by playing computer games (MacGonigal 2011) or that there would be "fun ways to cure cancer" (Scott 2013). An appreciation of statements like these necessitates a liaison between the ludic and empirical reality, and results in a state where "real life is becoming indistinguishable from computer games" to paraphrase a famous statement from Horkheimer and Adorno about movies (Adorno and Horkheimer 1993).

From Friedrich Schiller to Al Gore

Al Gore's before mentioned declaration of the normality of computer games is rooted in a philosophical tradition that tries to enoble playfulness as a universal source, medium or pharmakon of culture (Huizinga 1938). Friedrich Schiller's claim about humans being human only when playing[4] neglects non-ludic activities of men and women that constitute the human "in the fullest sense of the word" (Schiller 2013). To be able to work, sleep, love and hate without any playfulness in mind makes humans human. The inevitability of dying and the uncertainty about the time of death constitute humans in the fullest sense of the word as well. Markus Rautzenberg (this volume) refers to Jacques Lacan when he points out that it is not of course "uncertain if we die or not but that we live *as if* that was the case". Play might create situations that suggest certainty, but only within *de facto* uncertainty. This becomes apparent in the experiments on confidence, trust and unconsciousness that Karen Palmer stages brilliantly in her ludic performance *SYNCSELF 2* (2014). The *parkour* runner is challenged by uncertainty about the success of the next leap he or she is going to undertake. Will the concrete wall he or she is

---

4   "For, to speak out once for all, man only plays when in the full meaning of the word he is a man, and he is only completely a man when he plays" (Schiller 2013).

trying to reach crumble? Will he or she slip because of unforeseen moisture on the ground? Will a sudden gust of wind change the direction of the leap by a few crucial millimeters? The physical environment that *parkour* runners are acting in is loaded with uncertainty and with true randomness that a computer game is incapable of providing. Of course, the consequences of failing are of a different nature in the concrete (in both meanings of the word) world of parkour and the simulated physicality of worlds like the ones we know from *Assassin's Creed* (2007) and the like. The way the runner can accomplish a subjective feeling of certainty about his or her leap is by "framing the uncertainty" (Rautzenberg, this volume) as a game.

I wouldn't go as far as Espen Aarseth when, in an interview once, he stated that the only two conditions that could not be played are sleeping and dying (Aarseth 2009). I would contend that labour is another other human condition that cannot be played. I can of course imitate actions that are reminiscent of work and play a game of *mimicry* (Caillois 1958). But this does not play labour. Bataille states that the regime of labour denies play, and Robert Pfaller's reading of Bataille comes to the conclusion that "it does not do so by chance, it is the very nature of labour to be the negative of play" (Pfaller 2010, 20). Hammering on rocks on a theatre stage is therefore just a game about work-related symptoms, but it is not playing work at a substantial level.

For the idealist philosophy of Schiller, death and labour did of course matter less than beauty (*Schönheit*) and living form (*lebende Gestalt*). In the fifteenth letter on aesthetic education, Schiller suggests to closely relate "real and existing beauty" with the "real and existing drive for play" and goes as far as saying that the "ideal of beauty" dictates the "ideal of play" (Schiller 2013, 62). According to Schiller play has to be noble, bloodless and appreciable.

> We can immediately understand why the ideal form of a
> Venus, of a Juno, and of an Apollo, is to be sought not at

Rome, but in Greece, if we contrast the Greek population, delighting in the bloodless athletic contests of boxing, racing, and intellectual rivalry at Olympia, with the Roman people gloating over the agony of a gladiator.[5] (Schiller 2013, 62)

Obviously for Schiller there are good games and bad games!

What Schiller tries to accomplish in his *Letters on Aesthetic Education* (1795) is to declare play as the essential super-category encompassing and harmonising life and form. Life, according to Schiller, is the object of the sensual, bodily drives.[6] Gestalt is the object of the drive for form.[7] Both of those, the sensual drive and the form drive, exclude each other. That is why Schiller is searching for another drive, that he calls *Spieltrieb* (play drive) to aim at objects that could be labelled "*lebende Gestalt*", or "living form" (Schiller 2013, 58). Why?

> There shall be a communion between the formal impulse and the material impulse – that is, there shall be a play instinct – because it is only the unity of reality with the form, of the accidental with the necessary, of the passive state with freedom, that the conception of humanity is completed.[8] (Schiller 2013, 59)

5   German original: "Wenn sich die griechischen Völkerschaften in den Kampfspielen zu Olympia an den unblutigen Wettkämpfen der Kraft, der Schnelligkeit, der Gelenkigkeit und an dem edlern Wechselstreit der Talente ergötzen, und wenn das römische Volk an dem Todeskampf eines erlegten Gladiators oder seines lybischen Gegners sich labt, so wird aus diesem Zuge begreiflich, warum wir die Idealgestalten einer Venus, einer Juno, eines Apoll nicht in Rom, sondern in Griechenland suchen müssen" (Schiller 2013, 62).

6   German original: "Der Gegenstand des sinnlichen Triebes, in einem allgemeinen Begriff ausgedrückt, heißt Leben" (Schiller 2013, 58).

7   German original: "Der Gegenstand des Formtriebes, in einem allgemeinen Begriff ausgedrückt, heißt Gestalt" (Schiller 2013, 58).

8   German original: "Es soll eine Gemeinschaft zwischen Formtrieb und Stofftrieb, das heißt, ein Spieltrieb seyn, weil nur die Einheit der Realität mit der Form, der Zufälligkeit mit der Nothwendigkeit , des Leidens mit der Freyheit den Begriff der Menschheit vollendet" (Schiller 2013, 59).

Note the language. Schiller does not say that there is a unity of gestalt and life. He proclaims instead: "There shall be a communion between the formal impulse and the material impulse". Play and the play drive are constructed in order to optimise the ideal of humanity. That is why idealised play has to become normal and corrupted play (for example, the Romans and their Circus Maximus) or non-play has to be relegated to a second-class activity. It took some 230 years for Al Gore to arrive at a similar proposition: games are the new normal. Implicitly they are declared to be of prime importance and to be the only important human occupation.

From Diversity to Totality

The diversification of games can be seen as the maturing of the medium. The popularity of games has increased dramatically, games have become much more diverse and gaming is taking place in a wide range of practices, from e-sport to gamification. In addition, the gamer position includes a number of roles and identities such as: players, learners, time-fillers, users, fans, roleplayers, theory crafters, speed runners, and many more. Yet, the integration of games into everyday life absorbs the variety that once constituted the medium's strength. The more advanced the integration the more it turns into a mere spinning of gears. One might argue that the extension of play into all kinds of non-gaming contexts leads to an over-accumulation of play.[9] This is to suggest that play loses its liberating dynamics and becomes characterised by a quantitative increase of games and gaming, to a point of saturation. A situation could arise where the system's capacity to cope with further increase of playfulness is exhausted. This might lead to a qualitative leap that turns diversity into totality, and free play into total play. As a perversion

9   Schell used to call the over-accumulation "over-gamification" in his talk at
     the DICE summit in 2010 where he sketches an Orwellian scenario (Schell
     2010).

14   of the original play drive that is sensuous, liberating and free, a
model of total gamification could be prefigured by a conception
of games as the new normal and in which games are the only
normal. Exclusive normality leads to totality. Total gamification
would describe a situation where all human and technical
resources have to be gamified. In regards to human resources we
are already facing a situation where the old and the young, men
and women, various ethnic groups and a huge reserve army of
minorities and niche populations are drawn into gaming arenas.
The main games industries work with their brothers in arms of
the indie games industry to incessantly recruit new audiences:
the homeless, black teenage mums, those with depression or
Alzheimer's. But also on a technical level total Gamification takes
its toll. In his essay *"Gamification as the Post-Modern Phalanstère"*
Flavio Escribano describes a sector of gamification that he calls
"technological gamification" (Escibano 2012, 206–7). This is a type
of gamification that is triggered and driven by technological
innovation.[10] Escribano describes how large-scale simulations,
medical research, sports training, or military operations are run
on games technology to benefit from gaming's ease of use, low
cost, efficiency, legal status and design appeal.

The legitimisation for games being the "new normal" or the pick
of the day is not social desirability, but a new mode of power. Alex
Gekker calls this mode of technology-supported power "casual
power". His understanding of the concept relies on "designers
inscribing certain affordances into sociotechnical assemblages
that aim to nullify users' reflexive capacities towards the object in
question and enhancing its black-boxed condition" (Gekker 2015,
1). As soon as games are accepted as normal the question of why
they are played at a certain point in time and at a certain place by
certain people is not asked any longer. It is the alleged normality

---

10   Technological gamification differs from what Escribano calls "natural
gamification" and "forced gamification" as it is accepted on the basis of a
hegemonic status of technology versus other forms of knowledge or belief
(Escribano 2012, 203–6).

that keeps players and non-players alike from asking the question. Casual power transforms quotidian realities of everyday users, supplementing thinking or pre-thinking with suggested actions (Berry 2014).

The rationale of total gamification can be compared to the rationale of total mobilisation that was introduced by the director of German electric company AEG, Walther Rathenau and by General Erich Ludendorff one hundred years ago. Both for industrial resources and human resources (Ludendorff 1935) total mobilisation was demanded to progress in the war.[11] The request was not only to have more soldiers to fight, but to extend the resources for production and warfare to non-Germans, to women and to the youth.[12] Thirty years later Goebbels specified quite clearly what he had in mind when talking about the prospective participants of a total war: invalids from the eastern front, men and women working in the military industry, medical staff, scientists, artists, teachers, women, the young and the extremely old.[13] The expansion of core human resources to include a wide and diverse range of age groups, ethnicities and genders sounds like a target audience analysis by a gamification consultant of the twenty-first century. I do not, of course, want to say here that gamification is of the same nature as total mobilisation or even

---

11   In an even more brutal form Joseph Goebbels pronounced "total war" in his speech at the Berlin Sportpalast on February 18, 1943. Once more, a concentration and mobilisation of human resources (women and children) and of technology was asked for to progress the war in a state of allegedly temporary crisis. "The crises that our east front is momentarily suffering from" (translation by the author, German original: "Die Krise, in der sich unsere Ostfront augenblicklich befindet").

12   Cf. Imbusch (2005, 526), who identifies the following elements of total war: total mobilisation, total control, totality of methods, totality of the aims and objectives.

13   Translation by the author, German original: "deutsche Verwundete von der Ostfront [...] Rüstungsarbeiter und -arbeiterinnen aus den Berliner Panzerwerken, Ärzte, Wissenschaftler, Künstler, Lehrer [...] Über das ganze Rund des Sportpalastes verteilt sehe ich Tausende von deutschen Frauen. Die Jugend ist hier vertreten und das Greisenalter".

total war. It is, however, quite striking how the radical integration of broader audiences into serious gaming and the radicality of wartime recruitment follow similar rhetorics. Evangelists of gamification like McGonigal (2011) talk about "gaming as a spiritual practice", others pretend that "gamification design is largely about what is pleasureable" (Schell 2010)[14] and obscure economic objectives and interest. Erich Ludendorff talks about the "spiritual unity of the people"[15] and obscures the firing quota that he aims at in the first instance.

I have to clarify here, that I do not think that the current state of gamification has already reached a level of societal permeation that would justify talk of total gamification at the present time. What I have tried to point out is a tendency or a risk for the liberating power of playfulness to turn into a doctrine. In a situation like this it is so much more important to point out lines of flight from a totality of play. This is exactly what the authors of this book are concerned about.

Karen Palmer draws lines of flight for bodies and brains to escape traps. Tanya Krzywinska opens the discourse of playfulness towards the uncanny and the dark when she talks about the gamification of Gothic. Astrid Ensslin makes us aware of the power of narratives when we deal with worlds that are often mistaken as visual worlds, and the philosopher Markus Rautzenberg casts a critical glance at essentialisms that prevent us from looking for exceptions, uncertainties or the lack of supposed uncertainties.

14 Schell ideologises gamification by saying: "We are moving from a time when life was all about survival to a time when it was about efficiency into a new era where gamification design is largely about what is pleasureable" (Schell 2010).

15 German original: "Seelische Geschlossenheit des Volkes" (Ludendorff 1935).

Bibliography

Aarseth, Espen. 2009. *Unpublished Interview with Espen Aarseth by Mathias Fuchs* (December 3). Potsdam Hotel, Altstadt.

Adorno, Theodor, and Max Horkheimer. 1993. "The Culture Industry: Enlightenment as Mass Deception". In *Dialectic of Enlightenment*. New York: Continuum.

Adorno, Theodor. 2004. *Aesthetic Theory*. London: Continuum.

Berry, David M. 2014. *Critical Theory and the Digital: Critical Theory and Contemporary Society*. London: Bloomsbury.

Caillois, Roland. 1958. *Les jeux et les hommes*. Paris: Librairies Gallimard.

Ensslin, Astrid. 2015. "Keynote-Sprecherin Astrid Ensslin im Interview". Accessed June 25, 2015. http://cdc.leuphana.com/news/news/blog-article/interviewserie-digra2015-gothic-games-und-erste-spiele-keynote-sprecherin-astrid-ensslin-im-in/

Escribano, Flavio. 2012. "Gamification as the Post-Modern Phalanstère". In *The Video Game Industry*, edited by Peter Zackariasson and Timothy L. Wilson, 198–217. London: Routledge.

Gekker, Alex. 2015. *"Casual Power: Understanding User Interfaces through Quantification"*. Unpublished extended abstract for DiGRA2015. Lüneburg: DiGRA Abstracts.

Gore, Albert Arnold. 2011. "Keynote Lecture". *Eighth* Annual Games for Change Festival (June 20). New York.

Huizinga, Johan. (1938) 1985. *Homo Ludens: Proeve Ener Bepaling Van Het Spelelement Der Cultuur*. Reprint, Groningen: Wolters-Noordhoff.

Imbusch, Peter. 2005. *Moderne und Gewalt: Zivilisationstheoretische Perspektiven auf das 20. Jahrhundert*. Berlin: VS Verlag.

Ludendorff, Erich. 1935. *Der Totale Krieg*. München: Ludendorff's Verlag.

McGonigal, Jane. 2011. "Gaming as a Spiritual Practice". *Buddhist Geeks Podcast* 205. Accessed June 19, 2015. http://www.buddhistgeeks.com/2011/01/bg-205-gaming-as-a-spiritual-practice/.

Pfaller, Robert. 2010. "Der Exzess des Spiels als Begünder der Kultur". In *Das Spiel und seine Grenzen. Passagen des Spiels II*, edited by Mathias Fuchs and Ernst Strouhal, 9–30. Vienna and New York: Springer.

Rancière, Jacques. 2008. *Ist Kunst widerständig?* Berlin: Merve.

Schell, Jesse. 2010. *"Design Outside the Box"*. *DICE2010 Summit (February 18)*. Las Vegas. Accessed June 19, 2015. http://www.g4tv.com/videos/44277/dice-2010-design-outside-the-box-presentation/.

Schiller, Friedrich. 2013. *Über die ästhetische Erziehung des Menschen in einer Reihe von Briefen*. Stuttgart: Reclam.

Scott, Hilda. 2013. "Amazon, Facebook and Google Design Fun Way to Cure Cancer". In *Reuters/iTechPost* (March 1). Accessed June 19, 2015. http://www.itechpost.com/articles/5935/20130301/amazon-facebook-google-design-game-cure-cancer-research-uk.htm

Ludography

Angry Birds (2009). Rovio Entertainment.

Assassin's Creed (2007). Ubisoft.

SYNCSELF 2 (2014). Karen Palmer and If Interactive Film.

Gamification of Gothic

Tanya Krzywinska

Gothic themes, characters, stories, and environments can be found across a wide range of videogames, from puzzle games to multiplayer online games, and from shoot 'em ups to strategy games. With so many games drawing on the Gothic, why haven't game scholars been asking why games so frequently call upon it? Is this simply symptomatic of a decline in a humanities' approach to games and culture generally? More wide-ranging and focused work is certainly required as there is a major lack of sustained scholarly engagement with Gothic in videogames.[1] In an effort to begin the task of remedying this, and as part of a more extensive project,[2] this paper plots some initial coordinates of the domain, locating some of its major features, and provides a framework for evaluating the uses of Gothic in games. My

[1]   While there is work focused specifically on horror games, such as Perron's collection *Horror Video Games* (2009), there is no book or edited collection on the topic of Gothic in games. The author has, however, written several articles on the Gothic in games including entries in Blackwell guides to the Gothic.

[2]   The author is currently working on a book entitled *Gothic Games* (forthcoming).

underlying agenda here is that a Gothic perspective on games provides a methodology that enables sharper critical insight into the aesthetic and pleasure economies of games. Under the shield of humanities I bring together Game Studies with Gothic Studies, both of which share an attentiveness to the formation and reception of certain types of texts and their "meaning potential". Game studies and Gothic studies both carry and are constitutive of culture, and are laden with signification and organised around patterns. As Mikko Lehtonen puts it, "texts are not stuck on top of the rest of the world, as messages detachable from it, but participate in a central way in the making of reality as well as forming our image of it" (2000, 11). Gothic Studies evaluates texts, the way they are used and engaged with across a range of media and cultural practices. Game Studies focuses specifically on the formal specificities of games and the way they are played and engaged with. This paper calls on material from both provinces to fulfil its aim of understanding how videogame media shape the constitution of Gothic and my conviction that games have the capacity to add a new dimension to Gothic fiction's arsenal of affects. This is therefore a paper that pivots on the verb "gamification", which becomes therefore "remediation": describing the process of adapting a text, activity, genre, mode or style into game form. While this paper takes the position that Gothic is always rhetorically constituted, it claims there are more coherent claims on the nomenclature of Gothic than others, and that these must be identified if we are to understand in what form Gothic appears (or disappears) in games.

Scholarly work on videogames has grown apace since the first flush of books and articles came out in the early 2000s. Setting out the terms of this new field of academic study meant that much of the foundational work adopted a generalist approach by necessity. Espen Aarseth (2003) and Jesper Juul (2001) for example focused on what was common to all videogames and in so doing privileged computing, rules and game mechanics over the descriptive, adjectival and representational aspects of games. By contrast Janet Murray (2001, 2003) focused on games as story-based "cyberdramatic experiences", an approach that helped spark the "narratology/ludology" debate.[3] So dominant did this debate become that it obscured or discouraged other approaches to the academic study of games within the arts and humanities. This preoccupation with the (problematic) relationships between game rules and story, mechanics and representation, alongside the aspiration to ascertain the universal principles of videogames, left little scope for the investigation of more niche aspects. The situation was further intensified by the denouncement of work that mapped older methods and concepts, such as those developed within literature or film studies, onto games. Ignoring the value of comparative media analysis, Markku Eskelinen (2001) and Espen Aarseth (2003) pronounced that such endeavour ignored what was radically new and different about the medium of videogames.[4] This combative milieu, where rhetoric served the creation of opposing poles, was not favourable to the study of something so *apparently* narratological and representational as the presence of Gothic in games, even though aspects of it appeared in a range of well-known commercial games around that time.[5]

More conducive to the study of Gothic in games is a "textual" approach, notably Marie Laure Ryan's work on immersive,

---

3   Ludologists claimed that game mechanics were what defined games, not story. Now, most game scholars regard stories (where they are present) as important elements of the game-play experience that give meaning to the procedural elements of games. For a useful précis of the narratology/ludology debate and the building blocks of Game Studies see *First Person: New Media as Story, Performance and Game* (Wardrip-Fruin and Harrigan 2004).

4   An odd stance to take as a comparative approach has proved very useful in efforts to reveal what is new and different, as is evident, for example, in Henry Jenkins' work on transmediality and media convergence (2006) and that undertaken more generally within the Comparative Media Centre at MIT.

5   Examples include *Phantasmagoria* (1995), *Myst (1993)* and *Return to Castle Wolfenstein* (2001).

interactive worlds as texts (2001). Craig Lindley (2002) too advocated a more holistic approach to games, seeing story, rules and mechanics as unified whole, an approach echoed in Barry Atkins' *More Than a Game* (2003). Building on their earlier work and applying Roland Barthes' expanded notion of cultural artefacts as text, the introduction to *Videogame, Player, Text* (Atkins and Krzywinska, 2007) argued for the textual analysis of games. They did so not just in terms of story and representational gambits, but claimed code, rules and mechanics as intrinsic to the creation of games as "readable" textual artefacts. I would add that "reading" is often an integral part of playing a game, thereby acting itself as a core game mechanic. Atkins and Krzywinska also noted that games require a player/reader to kick them into action, thereby activating the semiotic, kinetic and affective energies that constitute player experience. Diane Carr extends this text/player synergy by arguing for the importance of taking into account the situated nature of play (2007), an idea developed more sharply in her work on disability and games (2013) which concentrates on the embodied player and the differences in play through the particularity of that embodiment. [6] Graeme Kirkpatrick argues for a balance between semiosis and experience, suggesting that fixing exclusively on the "meaning" of games elides the fact that our pleasure in playing games, as with playing with a ball, may originate in something more plastic: "Video games do not have to 'mean' anything to be popular and their popularity can be intelligible without reference to interpretation" (2011, 17). The sum of such scholarship provides a more nuanced understanding of the complex relations between videogame, player and text, and it is symptomatic that the analysis in this paper attends to the experiential "doing" element of what it is to play a game in order to make its argument that games have the capacity to bring a

[6] As well providing a framework for uncovering some of the normative assumptions of earlier work on games, and indeed in terms of games themselves, Carr's work on ability and disability is also highly relevant to the articulation of the Gothic in videogames.

new dimension to Gothic - even if that capability is by no means fully realised. A more rounded approach to the study of games is preferred because it takes into account how games are made, how they are played and how they draw on and are constitutive of culture. Most importantly, the textual analysis deployed within this paper allows us to evaluate the types of intertextual patterns and rhythms used to produce and articulate Gothic in games. It further permits evaluation of the impact the character-istic features of digital games (such as interactive, cybernetic, haptic, kinetic and embodied dimensions) have on the way Gothic is actualised ludically. The movement away from an exclusive rules-centric take on ludology (the study of games) towards more diverse approaches has widened the horizon of Game Studies, thereby enabling work that is more focused on individual games and genres, as well as on topics such as gender and philosophy. This extended range provides the scope required for a study of Gothic gamification.

Every game is comprised of systems that define and manage a player's actions. Most videogames possess an interface and are composed of rules, progress arcs, and winning conditions. Each game tailors these elements according to its own design logic which in turn governs the disposition of a game's spatiality and perspective. Therefore, to progress within a game, a player must actively engage with the particular demands set for him or her by the design of a game's mechanics. These mechanics range from the simple to the complex, encompassing what a player has to do in a game as well as the various elements of computing behind delivering the interface controls and the game to the screen. The specific horizon of interactivity, the particular scope of feedback mechanisms, and the precise arrangement of the interface configure around the overarching game concept. In addition to the characteristics of a given gaming platform and the market intended for that game, all these factors play a critical role in the particular way that a game "gamifies" Gothic. It is methodological consideration of these elements that provides part of the framework for critical evaluation.

Constructing a systematic theorisation of how the primary elements of a game treat their Gothic subject only proves productive and transcends taxonomy if an *evaluation* of that treatment is framed by a notional and coordinating sense of what is meant by Gothic. I began this work with an intuitive sense that there are vast variations in the effective, and indeed affective, uses of Gothic in games, and as work for this study progressed, that sense has intensified. Definition is therefore no simple task, especially considering that Gothic has spanned such a breadth of mood, time and location As Fred Botting notes "[t]he diffusion of Gothic forms and figures [...] makes the definition of a homogeneous generic category very difficult" (1996, 14). In his discussion of the uncertainty in scholarly definitions of the Gothic, David Punter writes that there is a "significant resistance to canonization" (2000, ix), suggesting that there is no one text that substantiates Gothic. It is therefore largely agreed within recent scholarship on the topic that Gothic is brimful of vertiginous, acute tangents and perplexing ambiguities. While Platonic ideals are overly confining, it is nonetheless necessary to pin-up some principles if we're to grasp what Gothic means for games. I do this from a broadly structuralist premise: games have a grammar. Game makers select elements from an established game grammar to construct a specific vocabulary for their game. The same can be said of Gothic. As with games, a set of conventions emerge cumulatively and proliferate from similar texts, sounding the structural beat to which story, style and theme dance. This does not mean an individual convention is stable or foundational however, and we can make useful application here of the structuralist axis of substitution and the plasticity that this affords to any meaning-producing system.[7] A radical change to the overall

7   Applying with some caveats Saussure's axes of langue and parole to genre, Rick Altman writes, "language is ... dependent on a different selection of paroles" (1999, 174).

pattern leads to hybridity and unfamiliarity (and in some cases creates a change in grammar). Patrick Kennedy (n.d.) provides a historically and visually aware definition of Gothic into which core renderings of otherness and affect are folded: Gothic "employs dark and picturesque scenery, startling melodramatic devices, and an overall atmosphere of exoticism, mystery and dread" (Kennedy n.d.). From here we can ask what the formal properties of games bring.

Gothic's capacity for constant and definition-bruising reinvention is evident through the ease of its adaptation into game form. Alongside Science Fiction, Gothic vocabulary is very commonly called upon by game developers making digital, blended (part digital) and other types of games (card, board, live-action and table-top games). It is perhaps most fully present in games that seek the status of art and pursue the creation of an experience of the sublime, such as *The Path* (2009) and *Dear Esther* (2012). It is also present in those games that utilise the sensationalist qualities of the supernatural to provoke a brooding sense of dread from *a player*, such as the case with the *Silent Hill* series (1999–present), *Fatal Frame* (2002), and *Dead Space* (2008). Gothic tropes also appear in games that do not seek primarily to dis-comfort players and which may be best defined as "cute", as is the case with *A Vampyre Story* (2008) or the *Burtonesque MediEvil* (1988). With these games we have to scrutinise the function of their Gothic elements to evaluate their relationship with Gothic. Gothic is best regarded as central to a games overall concept where Gothic themes and devices are woven into story, game mechanics and representational style. In other games, rep-resentation and iconography might draw directly on Gothic but cannot be said to pervasively inform gameplay and/or story. *The Secret of Monkey Island* (1990) for instance makes use of the supernatural and Gothic tropes but any potential for Gothic affect is lost in favour of light-hearted playfulness. Investigating the edges of Gothic, where style might not be underpinned by a more pervasive means of producing the affect of apprehension, shows how Gothic can be used to better understand games, as well as the conditions for its remediation in a game context.

Gothic Coordinates

Here I will propose five major coordinating nodes of Gothic in relation to games: character/story patterns; *mise-en-scène* and style; affect; entropy and sublime. Gothic is found in the way that these elements are handled or deployed. We can use these to evaluate the coherence of Gothic conventions (to pun on Sedgwick (1986)), as recipe for construction, or, as a method of critical appraisal.

An obliging place to start is the effect of Gothic on character and story patterns. Manuel Aguirre argues that Mary Shelley's *Frankenstein* (1818) makes use of the structural components of the hero's tale, reconfigured to stage the alternative journey of the "false hero"; "a hero who is not a hero" (2013, 11), the one who fails, who succumbs to entropy, the figure of tragedy.[8] The presence of this structural pattern and its particular reconfiguration provides our first major coordinate for defining and evaluating Gothic in games.[9] As Aguirre puts it, "Gothic abides by fairy tale narrative rules; it is only that Gothic individual who crosses over into the Other is no real hero [...] A key to Gothic thus resides in its centering the flawed character as protagonist [while] the standard hero of traditional tales is often demoted to a helpless or passive stance" (2013, 11). This latter point benchmarks a structural patterning that appears in relation to themes and economies of agency in a range of Gothic games and which provides a pivotal node in the process of judging whether the use of the grammar is simply replication or innovation. Examples

8   For the purposes of this essay, the hero and the false hero *could* be either male or female.

9   *Warcraft* (1994) and *World of Warcraft (2004–present)* players might recognise Arthas' journey from hero to false hero as one way that this game calls on and makes use of the Gothic.

of games drawing on false hero structures include *American*
McGee's Alice (2000), *Planescape Torment* (1999), *Shadow of the*
Colossus (2005/2006) and indie platformer *Limbo* (2010) as well as
roguelike *The Binding of Isaac* (2011). The "false hero" is therefore
emblematic of our first coordinate.

Our second coordinate is a particular use of *mise-en-scène*
(and by extension visual style) which can be symptomatic and
spatially locative of the journey of the "false hero". Haunted,
disquieted and uncanny spaces abound as "representations of
estrangement" made strange not by some property of the space
itself but as products of the cultural imagination (Vidler 1992,
12). Numerous games make use of Gothic locations, typically
haunted houses, spooky woods, crypts and graveyards, derelict
buildings, attics and cellars, without recourse to the "false hero"
pattern, begging a question about the strength of a given game
text's claim on Gothic. Here we might include the common use
of chiaroscuro, strong-contrast lighting to create visual drama,
perhaps emblematic of an occulted moral order, or low-contrast
lighting and/or muted colours to create a sense of grim griminess
serving often to illustrate ruin or decay. Colour is important in the
creation of Gothic atmospheres alongside baroque architectures,
labyrinths, ruins and decay, and a strong sense of isolation. In
addition, scenery that provides a strong sense of drama through
relative scale as provided by the mountains and abysses encoun-
tered by the heroine of Radcliffe's seminal Gothic novel *The Mysteries of Udolpho* (1794) and echoed, for example, in *The Shadow of
the Colossus*. This latter feature locks-in perfectly with coordinate
five. Many games made using 3D modelling tools create discrete
objects for placement within the game field. These objects are
therefore very heavily described and in some ways fighting
against the ambiguity and spectrality expected of Gothic; particle
effects therefore are commonly used in games that call on Gothic
to make geometry – and therefore the visual plane – less solid
and indeterminate.

The mode of representation, best termed "style", encompasses the aesthetic choices made in the realisation of *mise-en-scène*, the types of adjectives used, the objects chosen and used or the type of lighting for example. Style also includes the aesthetic rationale behind the choices made to organise the delivery of a story and is therefore manifest through editing, phrasing, elisions, use of time, auditory or visual elements, such as colour palette. It is important to note that it is not so much the individual components in themselves that comprise Gothic, but how these form patterns and how those patterns draw on the 'word-hoard' of previous Gothic texts and artefacts. Style and *mise-en-scène* commonly come together to produce indirect, environmental story-telling in the context of games. This mode of delivery is linked to a player's traversal of the game space and contributes to the creation of a stronger sense of presence within the game world for a player, thereby providing a foundation potentially for the generation of affect.

Out of such configurations emerge different flavours of Gothic that have their own distinctive patterns: fairy tale Gothic, Victorian Gothic, American Gothic or (even) Weird Gothic, for instance. These patterns might be juxtaposed with other generic, affective or stylistic patterns to form hybrids or to create meaning through difference; Martin Wills, for example, argues that "Dickens uses Gothic to isolate certain spaces to mark them off" (2012, 22). In addition to which, there may be a largely uniform Gothic style yet with no use of a Gothic "false hero", or there may a Gothic treatment of a genre. There are therefore games that use some aspects of Gothic, demonstrating the value of Wills' exhortation that, "[i]t is not *where* Gothic might be found that is important by *why* it is found, what it is employed to do" (Wills, 17; emphasis in original). Function therefore provides our fifth coordinate, helping us to evaluate the potential uses of Gothic in games; for example, localised use of Gothic helps reinforce the value of "home" in *Lord of the Rings Online* (2007–present), as it does in Tolkien's works. Gothic is used in *World of Warcraft*

(2004) through the Undead race to demonstrate moral relativism and, in a different context, provides the means to fuse together an ambiguous mix of power and objectification in *Bayonetta* (2009/2010). Function is then our third coordinate.

Our fourth coordinate is the representation, simulation and/ or production of a related group of psychologically affective emotional states: paralysis, claustrophobia, vertigo, alienation, estrangement, dread, discomfort and disorientation. Games often attempt to provoke such feelings for players and these may arise logically in some cases from game mechanics and story type, aligned often to the return-of-the-repressed structure as well as through the particular deployments of elements of *mise-en-scène*. Like adventure, comedy or romance, Gothic fiction carries a certain affective expectation, although many games that make cursory use of Gothic tropes have no intention to create a pervasive Gothic affect. In the context of games, incapacity, dread and claustrophobia (often rendered as a form of live burial) translate into the dimension of performance. In this sense Gothic redacts agency, using it to create sensation. Certainly sound also plays its role in heightening sensation, often helping to intensify panic or confusion. Games such as *Silent Hill* famously use sound to confuse and alienate, working against spatial and harmonious expectation to grate and grind on the player; fog is used to give a very palpable sense of claustrophobia, disabling the player from being prepared for what is coming and redacting the scope of player agency. The "dread" mechanic is also becoming a feature of Gothic-informed games, wherein events paralyse the player-character, as in *Call of Cthulhu: Dark Corners of the Earth (2006)* and *Lord of the Rings Online*. A Gothic game aesthetic is therefore correlated directly and powerfully with players through the (in) ability to perform.

> And then a Plank in Reason, broke,
> And I dropped down, and down –
> And hit a World, at every plunge,

And finished knowing – then –
        "I felt a Funeral, in my brain" Emily Dickinson

Entropy and the sublime is our fifth coordinate. You might already detect a disjunction between Gothic and normative game grammar and we need a detour here to get to this fifth coordinate. Games and puzzles are built on the notion that there is a solution, a winning condition, and many games that we might easily call Gothic, such as the *Midnight Mysteries* (2009–2012) series, are therefore caught up within a polarisation between the normative vocabulary of games, where players are catalysts for redemption, and the intractable sense of loss and entropy that characterises Gothic. There are however different ways that winning can be treated and contextualised while still making use of generic game vocabulary, providing thereby a means to develop a specifically Gothic winning condition that grows out of story and function. Here winning would not be triumphant, but instead melancholy, experienced as a loss of something or someone, as occurs in *Primal* (2003) where Jen fails to save her boyfriend and loses something of the vulnerability that makes her human, allowing her, however, to survive in a metaphysically disturbed and physically hostile world. The total rejection of any winning condition does of course challenge the very definition of a game.

Games do, though, have their own occulted forces: AI and the logic-based machinations of an invisible computational layer, as well as the Skinnerist arrays of feedback from which games are constituted. These can be exploited thematically and textually towards entropic ends when placed in a pervasive Gothic context. This resonant and modally located consequence might also help to explain the popularity of Gothic in games. In a Gothic context, a game's algorithmic system potentially accrues a mysterious, godlike power that steers choice, behaviour and morality through arrays of determinants, and positive or negative reinforcements. This feature is used thematically and resonantly in *Bioshock* (2007) as well as in distinctly Gothic-Weird context of

The Stanley Parable (2011). The occulted layer that presides with
such potency over a player's actions and which determines the
extent and appropriateness of those actions provides then a key
for unlocking the potential of a special functional bond between
videogame form and Gothic, and which gives additional scope for
a player to experience, in a ludic sense, the position of the false
hero.

 "To act" (and to act in a timely and correct manner) is the leading
currency of interactive games and "to be unable to act" is Gothic
articulation, or perversion, of this currency in games. In *Call
of Cthulhu: Dark Corners of the Earth*, a player-character must
often run from situations rather than stand and fight. There is
no gun provided early in the game; no chance to prove yourself
an unconditional action hero. Following Lovecraft's pessimistic
mythos/ethos on which the game is based, the game places a
player-character as subject to events rather than their master.
This is symbolised by periods of madness and fear that inter-
fere with a player-character's ability to act. Core to creating the
sensation of claustrophobia, a palpable sense of vulnerability
is essential to Gothic's affective intent. In many games the
opposite pertains; for many players, pleasure is found in the
sense of invulnerability games generate. In the gendered eco-
nomics of popular culture, vulnerability is often represented by
a female character, which Carol Clover argues provides a means
of allowing men to experience fear safely at one remove (1992).
In some Gothic games, female characters are played against
gender tropes, that is, as skillful and resourceful: for example,
Alice of *American McGee's Alice* is highly rational and capable even
if the entire world has become irrational and nightmarish; while
Jen in *Primal* (2003) develops demonic attributes in her quest to
save her kidnapped boyfriend. In these cases there is an altered
relationship with power afforded by playing against gender
convention. The presence of a player-character as false hero is a
pivot on which a game can conjure a potent and pervasive Gothic
configuration and a method for understanding gaming norms.

34	Games are repeatedly sold to players as affording agency and
skill, where the deft practice of hand-eye coordination and acute
timeliness is rewarded with positive feedback; these work in
contradistinction to existential dread, claustrophobia, paralysing
fear, and an inability to act that are constitutive of Gothic.
Within the heroic and Vitruvian structure of many games, Gothic
elements are overcome and mastered: the Other is compart-
mentalised and projected outward, the real of the body and
difference subdued, and normative notions of human sovereignty
reinforced.

Death in real life is a curtailment of agency (even if the effects
of our acts might be felt after our demise). Many games deny
the finality of real death, and become simply a prompt for the
player to try harder to learn what the game requires for them to
progress. Death is functional in games, rather than sublime. It
is simply another feedback mechanism.[10] In most games we are
shown how we are defined by death: it is not entropic. A player-
character "dies" and returns in the most un-Gothic of ways; they
do not haunt the screen (although this might be said to be the
case in *Dark Souls 2 (2014)*).[11] In and of itself this return is literally
"canny" rather than uncanny – canny in the sense that you get to
retry and re-write your game history. In most games, and echoing
Freud's notion of the death drive (2003), a lack of progression is
constitutive of how death signifies – and only calls on the Gothic
because it redacts agency (*but* only temporarily and often as a
stage on the road of progress). As such, in most games, death
signifies non-metaphysically through an oscillating movement
between action and inaction, and from stasis to progress
(Krzywinska 2002). To prevail is to progress effectively, denying
the sublime entropy that gives Gothic its fearful symmetry.
The way in which death is realised, and how it is tied to a game
mechanics, has then an impact on the realisation of Gothic, and

10	Cf. Markus Rautzenberg's text in this book [editor's comment].
11	Thanks to Jack Hackett for drawing my attention to *Dark Souls 2*.

a game's claim on the nomenclature. I would offer the following: the more meaning and intensity assigned to death, the more intently are activated our five coordinates and therefore the more intently "Gothic" a game can be deemed to be.

Games often draw on Gothic as a "marketing tool for writers anxious to gain access to popular reading audiences" (Gamer 2000, 29). Such patterns are clearly useful for the game industry which has relied on clear communication with its target market to get a return on their development investment. In game terms the use of ritualised textual patterns also has the function of manifesting the "magic circle", Huizinga's term for the way that we enter a different mindset and social relation when playing a game (1971). In this sense the conflation of "Gothic" and "game" becomes a fast track means of constructing the space of the Other, but this doesn't necessarily imply transgression. The mutability of Gothic may well imply change and movement, but it also makes it a great commercial ally. This is why the treatment of otherness and entropy is so important, if we are to retain Gothic as a critical methodology. Entropy and otherness must there-fore be sutured into the fabric of the game through our other four coordinates. *This* Gothic can be mobilised to question reified assumptions and fictions that we use to shore up and solidify our existence and which are supported by the unproblematised agency and Vitruvian coordinates of many games. In some few videogames, with room for more, Gothic becomes a mode through which the very borders and capabilities of this new expressive medium can be explored. With their coded base easily manipulated by the cognoscenti, their branching narratives, and the provision in some cases of tools for adding to their content, games share with Gothic the appeal of collective myth and a type of immersion and participation that disturbs and transforms. Gothic pulls in a different direction from some of the normative features of videogames, particularly the idea that games can be "won" and where death equates to "trying again", yet games are nonetheless pregnant with Gothic potential because they are predicated on agency, performance and progress.

Acknowledgements: *An extended version of this essay can be found at The Revenant, an e-journal dedicated to academic and creative explorations of the supernatural, the uncanny and the weird.*

Bibliography

Aarseth, Espen. 1997. *Cybertext: Perspectives on Ergodic Literature*. New York: Johns Hopkins University Press.

Aarseth, Espen. 2003. "Playing Research: Methodological Approaches to Game Analysis". *Melbourne DAC, the Fifth Annual Digital Arts and Culture Conference* (May 19–23). Melbourne. Accessed June 20, 2015. http://hypertext.rmit.edu.au/dac/papers/Aarseth.pdf.

Aguirre, Manuel. 2013. "Gothic Fiction and Folk-Narrative Structure: The Case of Mary Shelley's Frankenstein". *Gothic Studies* 15 (2): 1–18.

Altman, Rick. 1999. *Film/Genre*. London: BFI.

Atkins, Barry. 2003. *More Than A Game: The Computer Game as Fictional Form*. Manchester: Manchester University Press.

Atkins, Barry, and Tanya Krzywinska. 2007. *Videogame, Player, Text*. Manchester: Manchester University Press.

Botting, Fred. 1996. *Gothic*. London: Routledge.

Carr, Diane. 2007. "Un-situated Play: Textual Analysis and Videogames". *Hardcore* on the Digital Games Research Association website. Accessed June 20, 2015. http://www.digra.org/hardcore-18-un-situated-play-textual-analysis-and-digital-games-diane-carr/.

Carr, Diane. 2013. "Digital Games: Representations of Ability and Disability Project Update". *Games Research Seminar* (December 2). University of London.

Clover, Carol J. 1992. *Men, Women, and Chainsaws*. Princeton: Princeton University Press.

Dickinson, Emily. 1998. *The Poems of Emily Dickinson: Variorum Edition*. Edited by Ralph W. Franklin. Cambridge, MA: The Belknap Press of Harvard University Press.

Eskelinen, Markku. 2001. "The Gaming Situation". *Game Studies* 1 (8). Accessed June 20, 2015. http://www.gamestudies.org/0101/eskelinen/.

Fernández-Vara, Clara. 2009. "The Secret of Monkey Island: Playing Between Cultures". In *Well Played 1.0: Video Games, Value and Meaning*, edited by Drew Davidson et al. Pittsburg: ETC Press. Accessed June 20, 2015. http://press.etc.cmu.edu/content/secret-monkey-island-clara-fern%C3%A1ndez-vara.

Freud, Sigmund. 2003. "Beyond the Pleasure Principle". In *Beyond the Pleasure Principle and Other Writings*. Harmondsworth: Penguin Books.

Gamer, Michael. 2000. *Romanticism and Gothic*. New York: Cambridge University Press.

Huizinga, John. 1971. *Homo Ludens*. Boston: Beacon Press.

Kennedy, Patrick. n.d. "Gothic Literature". *About.com*. Accessed June 20, 2015. http://literatureintranslation.about.com/od/definitions/g/Gothic-Literature.htm.

Lehtonen, Mikko. 2000. *The Cultural Analysis of Texts*. London: Sage Press.

Lindley, Craig A. 2002. "The Gameplay Gestalt, Narrative and Interactive Story-telling". In *Computer Games and Digital Cultures*, edited by Frans Mäyrä, 203–215. Tampere: Tampere University Press.

Jenkins, Henry. 2006. *Convergence Culture*. New York: New York University Press.

Juul, Jesper. 2001. "Games Telling Stories? A Brief Note on Games and Narratives". *Game Studies* 1 (1). Accessed June 20, 2015. http://www.gamestudies.org/0101/juul-gts/.

Juul, Jesper. 2003. "The Game, a Player, the World: Looking for the Heart of Gameness". In *Level Up: Digital Games Research Conference (November 4-6)*, edited by Marinka Copier and Joost Raessens, 30–45. Utrecht: Utrecht University.

King, Geoff, and Tanya Krzywinska, eds. 2002. *ScreenPlay: Cinema/Videogames/Interfaces*. London: Wallflower Press.

Kirkland, Ewan. 2009. "Storytelling in Survival Horror Videogames". In *Horror Video Games*, edited by Bernard Perron, 62–78. Jefferson: McGraw Hill.

Kirkpatrick, Graeme. 2011. *Aesthetic Theory and the Video Game*. Manchester: Manchester University Press.

Krzywinska, Tanya. 2002. "Hands-on Horror". In *ScreenPlay: Cinema/Videogames/Interfaces*, edited by Geoff King and Tanya Krzywinska, 206–233. London: Wallflower Press.

Krzywinska, Tanya. 2009. "Reanimating Lovecraft: The Ludic Paradox of *Call of Cthulhu: Dark Corners of the Earth*". In *Horror Video Games*, edited by Bernard Perron, 267–87. Jefferson: McGraw Hill.

Murray, Janet. 2001. *Hamlet on the Holodeck: The Future of Narrative in Cyberspace*. Cambridge, MA: MIT Press.

Murray, Janet. 2003. "What are Games Made Of?". In *Level Up: Digital Games Research Conference (November 4-6)*, edited by Marinka Copier and Joost Raessens. Utrecht: Utrecht University.

Perron, Bernard. 2009. "The Survival Horror: The Extended Body Genre". In *Horror Video Games*, edited by Bernard Perron, 121–43. Jefferson: McGraw Hill.

Sedgwick, Eve Kosofsky. 1986. *The Coherence of Gothic*. London: Methuen.

Shaviro, Steven. 1993. *The Cinematic Body*. Minneapolis: University of Minnesota Press.

Sontag, Susan. 1977. *On Photography*. Harmondsworth: Penguin Books.

Wardrip-Fruin, Noah, and Pat Harrigan. 2004. *First Person: New Media as Story, Performance and Game*. Cambridge, MA/London: MIT Press.

Wills, Martin. 2012. "Victorian Realism and Gothic: Objects of Terror Transformed". In *The Victorian Gothic: An Edinburgh Companion*, edited by Andrew Smith and William Hughes, 15–28. Edinburgh: Edinburgh University Press.

38   Vidler, Anthony. 1992. *The Architectural Uncanny*. Cambridge, MA: MIT Press.
Young, Philip. 1984. *Hawthorne's Secret: An Untold Tale*. Boston: David R Godine.

Ludography

A Vampyre Story (2008). Crimson Cow. Autumn Moon.

American McGee's Alice (2000). Rogue Entertainment. EA Games.

Bayonetta (2009/2010). Platinum. Sega.

Bioshock (2007). Irrational Games. 2K Games.

Burtonesque MediEvil (1988). SCEE.

Call of Cthulhu: Dark Corners of the Earth (2006). Headfirst. Ubisoft.

Dark Souls 2 (2014). From Software/Namco.

Dead Space (2008). EA Redwood/EA.

Dear Esther (2012). The Chinese Room.

Fatal Frame (2002). Tecmo. Wanadoo.

Limbo (2010). Playdead/Microsoft Game Studios.

Lord of the Rings Online (2007–present). Turbine, Inc. Warner Bros. Interactive
Entertainment.

Midnight Mysteries (2009–2012). MumboJumbo.

Myst (1993). Cyan Worlds/Presto Studios/Ubisoft. Brøderbund.

Phantasmagoria (1995). Sierra Online. Kronos.

Planescape Torment (1999). Black Isle Studios. Interplay Entertainment.

Return to Castle Wolfenstein (2001). Id. Activision.

Shadow of the Colossus (2005/2006). Team Ico. SCE Japan.

Silent Hill series (1999–present). KCET. Konami.

The Binding of Isaac (2011). Headup Games.

The Path (2009). Tale of Tales.

The Secret of Monkey Island (1990). Lucasfilm Games. LucasArts.

The Stanley Parable (2011). Davey Werden.

Warcraft (1994). Blizzard Entertainment.

World of Warcraft (2004–present). Blizzard Entertainment.

Video Games as Unnatural Narratives

Astrid Ensslin

Introduction

What I aim to undertake here is to approach video games from a territory within postclassical narratology hitherto largely untouched by ludologists. The study of unnatural narratives is one of the most recent fields within contemporary narrative theory and deeply intertwined with the endeavour to understand how human beings make sense of narrative texts and artefacts across media that cannot be sufficiently accounted for or analysed using traditional narratological theories (Alber et al. 2010, 113). So this article seeks to open up a new field of ludo-narratological enquiry targeted, in particular, at games that push ludo-narratological boundaries and call out for meta-ludic debate and reflection, albeit not necessarily with an avant-garde agenda in mind. In fact, the games that I'm going to look at in the analytical part of this study are commercially traded and played by global audiences, possibly because rather than despite the fact that they *prima facie* go against the grain, and call out for meta-ludic debate, specialised analytical tools and conceptual frameworks.

The idea for this project grew out of my previous monograph project on *Literary Gaming* (Ensslin 2014), which is situated at the junction between indie games, electronic literature and ludo-stylistic analysis. For this book I deliberately chose the title literary "gaming" rather than "games" because literary games proper (in the sense of games that embed literary structures and encourage literary reading interwoven with gameplay) are only one sub-form of what I see as a continuum between ludic digital literature (where literary reading is foregrounded and games and play are integrated in digital literary structures) and literary games as I've just described them. So in a nutshell, the study of literary gaming looks at hybrid digital media that combine different types of gameplay and literary reading which cause clashes and creative interplay between what Hayles (2007) calls "hyperattention" and "deep attention" in reader-players. Ludic forms of digital literature correlate mostly with the deep attentive side of the spectrum, while literary games are experienced in a mostly hyperattentive state.

The term literary gaming spans a wide range of ludo-literary media including poetry games,[1] literary/narrative auteur games,[2] interactive fiction,[3] ludic and meta-ludic types of hypertext and hypermedia,[4] as well as more linear ludo-literary digital narratives produced in Flash, Shockwave and other interactive

---

1   For example, by Jason Nelson, Jim Andrews and Gregory Weir.

2   For an explanation of this term, see Ensslin (2014). For examples of such games see those by Mike Bithell, Jonathan Blow, Tale of Tales, and Galactic Café/Davey Wreden.

3   For example, works by Nick Montfort, Emily Short and Aaron Reed.

4   For example, by geniwate, Deena Larsen, Robert Kendall and Richard Holeton.

animation technologies,[5] as well as navigable 3D literary
environments.[6]

This essay forms a first step towards my new book project
(co-authored with digital stylistician Alice Bell) called *Unnatural
Narratives and Digital Fiction* (Ensslin and Bell, forthcoming),
which applies theoretical and analytical concepts of unnatural
narratology to various types of digital fictions (including
hypertext fiction, Flash fiction, interactive fiction and narrative
games). I'm going to discuss some ways of understanding
unnaturalness in games, using two very different definitions of
the unnatural in comparison, and explore the extent to which
they may be useful to close analysis. I will begin by providing
some theoretical background on videogames' narrativity, on
unnatural narratives and unnatural narratology. I'll then move
on to a dual argument based on two divergent definitions of
unnaturalness: given a broad conceptual framework, I propose
that – in many ways – videogames are unnatural narratives
par excellence; therefore the term can be seen as somewhat
tautological when it comes to ludic narrativity.

Taking a more narrow, aesthetically oriented definition as a
starting point, I contend, in a second move, that some games are
more "unnatural" than others, and that the idiosyncratic ludo-
narrative mechanics exhibited by them allow us to apply, adapt
and further develop existing concepts and tools developed by
unnatural narratologists. In the analytical part of this essay I'll
then have a look at three games in particular that showcase some
key aspects of unnatural narratology at work: Tale of Tales' *The
Path* (2009), and its uses of unnatural spatiality, Jonathan Blow's
Braid (2009) and its uses of unnatural temporality and, finally,
Galactic Café's *The Stanley Parable* (2013) and its uses of unnatural
narration – in particular the role of the would-be omniscient

5   For example, works by Serge Bouchardon, Kate Pullinger and Christine
    Wilks.
6   For example, by Andy Campbell and Judi Alston.

narrator and his conflict with the player-character. In my closing remarks I'll sum up some of my initial conclusions about the relevance and feasibility of unnatural narratology for the study of games, and I'll make some suggestions as to how we may develop this analytical approach further to accommodate the media-specificity of digital games and gaming.

Ludo-narratological Assumptions

The ludo-narratological approach taken here is set against the background of what are by now widely agreed assumptions about the narrativity of games. First, a game isn't a *narrative* in the sense of a pre-scripted sequence of events, or indeed "any semiotic object produced with the intent of evoking a [pre-intended] narrative script in the mind of the audience" (Ryan 2004a, 9). Instead, they *possess narrativity*, as Marie-Laure Ryan puts it in *Narrative Across Media* (2004a, 9), which means that they have the potential to evoke multiple, individualised narrative scripts through settings, characters and other elements that players interact with through choice and with the intention to solve problems and make progress. Thus, in gameplay, users are turned into characters, and as players we enact the destiny, or the trajectory, of the game world *autotelically* (Ryan 2004a, 349), that is, through our own motivated actions rather than being told about or shown events as we are in fiction, drama or film.

- In a more detailed analysis, Henry Jenkins (2004) breaks the narrative properties of games into three core concepts:
- "Environmental storytelling" means that games are designed as environments, as worlds full of characters and props for players to interact with (much like Disney World and other amusement parks). Players explore games spatially, in an episodic way, and this nonlinear model is kept coherent by an overarching goal and repetitive mechanic. Games also form part of a larger storytelling ecology, which brings to mind Jenkins' (2006)

theory of transmedia storytelling, which assumes that stories develop and evolve across media, rather than simply being re-mediated or adapted). Finally, games are evocative spaces with large mnemonic potential in that they evoke the structures of existing stories and the genre traditions of other media.[7]

- "Emergent narratives" refers to the ways in which players create their own stories by exploring the game world (corresponding roughly to Ryan's (2004a) autotelic enactment). These stories become manifest in oral storytelling or participatory media, such as gamer fora or on YouTube, where gamers post their own playthroughs, walkthroughs, Let's Plays etc.

- "Embedded narratives", which are any non-interactive narrative sequences integrated into or surrounding gameplay, such as cut-scenes, backstory descriptions or dialogues (written or voiced-over). They tend to be embedded in such a way as not to impede the interactive flow of gameplay, and they may function as rewards or level-up markers; they may help drive the story forward or bridge loading time. Needless to say, their usefulness and aesthetic potential are controversial topics amongst gamers, and there are significant cultural differences with respect to accepted duration and player patience (Ensslin 2011, 166).

Arguably there's a lot more to say about videogame narrativity more generally, but I'll now move straight on to the core theoretical interest of this essay: the varying concepts of "unnatural" narrativity and how they may or may not contribute to understanding video games as ludo-narrative media.

---

7   For example, *Red Dead Redemption (2010)* vis-à-vis the Western genre, the
    Lego series, *Star Wars* or *Indiana Jones*.

Unnatural Narratives – Unnatural Narratology

Before embarking on an examination of what unnatural narratives are, it needs to be acknowledged that the term is highly evocative of numerous problematic meanings and uses: it carries ideology-ridden connotations of hegemonic "normality", of discursively constructed social and cultural hierarchies, and oppositions and binary thought more generally. Furthermore, the school of "unnatural narratologists" (much like that of "natural narratologists") is deeply rooted in western, Anglo-American scholarship, and the vast majority of texts studied under this theoretical umbrella are authored by Anglo-American writers, which leaves a large part of global narrativity unaccounted for. Finally, popular notions of "unnaturalness" are negatively connoted, as it is often used to "denounce certain types of behavior (as well as sexual orientations or practices) which the speaker considers to be deviant or perverse" (Alber and Heinze 2011, 2), and this of course adds to the controversy surrounding terminological choices underlying this theoretical apparatus.

Having said all that, the term "unnatural" as used by narratologists carries a highly specialised set of meanings, and can only be comprehended in the context of its derivation. It was borrowed from Monika Fludernik's idea of a "natural narratology", which is anchored in a cognitive approach to human experientiality and the ways in which narratives and narrativity can be re-evaluated from the point of view of "natural", or "naturally occurring" storytelling in the Labovian sense (1996, 13). So the derivate "unnatural" and its surrounding theories form a response to Fludernik's concept, and – despite its somewhat misleading negative prefix – the term needs to be understood in a distinctly positive, productive sense for purposes of cognitive narratological analysis:

> [t]he aim of an unnatural theoretical approach is to approx-
> imate and conceptualize Otherness, rather than to stigmatize
> or reify it; such an approach is interested in various kinds of
> narrative strangeness and in particular in texts that deviate
> from the mimetic norms of most narratological models.
> (Alber and Heinze 2011, 2)[8]

One of the most frequently quoted definitions of unnatural
narratives is by Jan Alber, who describes them as a "subset of
fictional narratives" (2013a). According to Alber (2013a) such a
narrative:

> violates physical laws, logical principles, or standard
> anthropomorphic limitations of knowledge by representing
> storytelling scenarios, narrators, characters, temporalities,
> or spaces that could not exist in the actual world.

In other words, unnaturalness is defined *ex negativo* in opposition
to the "natural" (see above), which relates to the cognitive frames
and scripts we have derived from our actual experience of being
in the world. So according to Alber's fairly broad and inclusive
notion, unnaturalness refers to both physically and logically
impossible narrative structures, which includes the supernatural
in fairy tales as much as it does, for example, multiple contradictory endings of a story, or two parallel timelines that unfold at
different speeds.

Another, more narrowly defined and aesthetically oriented concept of unnaturalness is put forward by Brian Richardson. To him,
unnatural narratives:

> conspicuously violate [...] conventions of standard narrative
> forms, in particular the conventions of nonfictional
> narratives, oral or written, and fictional modes like realism
> that model themselves on nonfictional narratives. Unnatural

---

8   Of course, the boundary between "natural" and "unnatural" isn't clear-cut;
    unnaturalness has to be understood as a matter of degree rather than an
    absolute quality.

narratives furthermore follow fluid, changing conventions and create new narratological patterns in each work. In a phrase, unnatural narratives produce a defamiliarization of the basic elements of narrative. (Richardson 2011, 34)[9]

Again, he defines unnaturalness *ex negativo* as narrative structures that are anti-mimetic, which means they are "clearly and strikingly impossible in the real world" (Alber et al. 2013, 102) and defy the principles of: (a) mimetic, realistic fictional story-telling, and; (b) the conventions of nonfictional narratives, oral and written for purposes of aesthetic innovation, critical pleasure and meta-level reflection (Richardson 2011, 34).

Hence, whereas Alber puts both physical and logical scenarios in one "unnatural" basket, Richardson makes a crucial distinction between so-called *non*-mimetic (or physically impossible or fantastic) and *anti*-mimetic narrative structures, which defy the principles of reality and realistic storytelling, but also the conventions of existing media genres we tend to be familiar with, and not in a deliberately negative, or alienating way, but rather in a creative, productive manner that engenders various types of reflective thinking in audiences.[10] Hence, Richardson's concept is geared more towards the audience's (projected or likely rather than empirically tested) response than a textual quality. What matters to him is "the degree of unexpectedness that the text produces, whether surprise, shock, or the wry smile that acknowledges that a different, playful kind of representation is at work" (Richardson 2015, 5).

The study of unnatural narratives, called unnatural narratology, is a subdomain of postclassical narratology (Herman 1999), which

9   Cf. Shklovsy (1965).
10   According to Alber, Richardson's "distinction between non- and anti-mimetic elements is identical with [his] distinction between conventionalized and not yet conventionalized instances of the unnatural" (Personal correspondence, May 30, 2015).

represents a departure from classical structuralist narratology[11] in that it is both transmedial and transdisciplinary:

1. It broadens the scope of analytical objects from print-based, literary fiction to narrative media more widely, as well as non-fictional forms of storytelling (in the Labovian tradition of oral storytelling).
2. It expands the narratologist's analytical and conceptual toolkit by integrating non-literary disciplines such as post-Saussurean linguistics (for example, discourse analysis, possible-worlds semantics etc.), gender theory, ethnography, cognitive science (schema and frames and scripts theory), film and media studies.

As far as its cross-media remit is concerned, unnatural narratology has reached out to drama, film, comics, nonfictional testimonies and hypertext fiction, but very little work exists (to my knowledge) that deals with the idiosyncratic narrativity of videogames. So this is where my theoretical and analytical contribution lies with this project.

It's not surprising that many, if not most, unnatural narratologists have looked at postmodernist narratives (novels, short stories, films) when developing their theories. So if I'm proposing in this essay that in many ways mainstream videogames are unnatural narratives *par excellence*, I'm doing something quite unconventional, or theoretically unnatural in its own right, because I'm arguing that "unnatural" is actually quite "natural" (or rather conventionalised) when it comes to videogames (according to Alber's definition), and that the body of games that we can meaningfully refer to and analyse as "unnatural" (using Richardson's definition) is still fairly small (but growing, and an exciting development to follow within the indie sector in particular).

When studying unnatural narratives, a core, classical narratological distinction is usually made between unnaturalness

11   Associated with Genette, Chatman, Bal and Prince.

at story level (which concerns the actual underlying fabula, or that which is told), and at discourse level (which is the level of the telling, that is, of narrative organisation, sequentialisation or design). So, for example, unnatural temporality at the story level happens in time-travel narratives (where the protagonist may criss-cross between different historical periods consecutively), whereas at discourse level the story may remain unaffected by discourse-level fragmentation, mixing or reversal, such as in Nolan's *Memento* (Heinze et al. 2013). For games, this distinction has to be substituted for by a concept that allows for the executability of the underlying code, and Jenkins's (2004) idea of emergent narrativity, where the player's interaction with the coded interface produces as many stories as there are players and playthroughs.

Reading Strategies and Conventionalisation

We've established earlier that unnaturalness can be understood in terms of unconventional and defamiliarising structures and experiences. Surely, however, what we've come to accept as "conventional" hasn't always been such: basic cognitive frames develop over time and the more often we're exposed to specific "impossible" scenarios, the more readily we'll integrate them into our repository of "the possible" – so we naturalise (Culler 1975) initially unfamiliar, or defamiliarising structures, by embedding them into our cognitive frames of reference. And these mental repositories of ours tend to be genre-bound. We've become used to, for example, speaking animals from fables, fairy tales and other types of fantasy (which are non-mimetic but not anti-mimetic according to Richardson), we've conventionalised the omnimentality of the omniscient narrator (which is a humanly impossible quality – no-one can know everything, least of all what other people are thinking exactly, but we've become used to it especially from classical realist novels), and we're perfectly well-accustomed to time-travel narratives (as they often occur in sci-fi) and physically impossible geographies such as flying islands.[12]

So why and how does conventionalisation happen? Essentially, it's within our human nature that, when we encounter anything unfamiliar, or strange, as we do in unnatural narratives, we try to make sense of it in some way, by applying a range of reading strategies. As Alber puts it, we are "ultimately bound by [our] cognitive architecture, even when trying to make sense of the unnatural. Hence, the only way to respond to narratives of all sorts (including unnatural ones) is through cognitive frames and scripts" (2013b, 451–54), so on the basis of cognitive theory, Alber proposes the following reading strategies employed by readers (in any combination and any order (cf. Alber 2013c, 49)) to help them "come to terms with the unnatural" (2013b, 451):

1. Frame blending: here we blend pre-existing frames that we previously considered to be incompatible (for example, that the flow of time may be tied to the direction in which you move, which is the case in world four ("Time and Place") of Braid).
2. Generification: evoking genre conventions from literary and media history. So here the blending has already happened and we've integrated it as a possible convention in a given genre or medium (for example, time travel in sci-fi narratives; or super-human jump heights in platformers).
3. Subjectification: here we attribute the unnatural to internal states, such as dreams, nightmares, or hallucinations. We know it's perfectly natural for our unconscious mind to produce highly surreal scenarios, so this option is part of our explanatory repository, especially when we're dealing with an unreliable narrator or a vulnerable, victimised protagonist (such as the six sisters in The Path, who all have to meet "their" wolf in the form of an age-specific traumatic experience).

---

12   Laputa in Swift's *Gulliver's Travels (1726)*.

4. Thematic foregrounding: here we identify specific thematic elements in a narrative that recur, in various configurations, to form an idée fixe (for example, the relationship between time and human experience, in Braid, or the meta-ludic conflicts in The Stanley Parable).

5. Allegorical reading: here we understand unnatural structures as part of an extended metaphor about the human condition, or the world in general. In this regard the impossibility of meaningful play in The Stanley Parable can be seen as an allegory of illusory agency (McCallum-Stewart and Parsler 2007) in gameplay more generally.

6. Satirisation and parody: this occurs when narratives try to mock either other narratives or elements of the world in general; the zero-player game Progress Quest for example is unnatural in that it doesn't allow players to do anything other than watch the game "play itself", thereby parodying massively multiplayer online games (MMOGs) such as Everquest (and particularly their auto-attack function, which is extremely passive).

7. Positing a transcendental realm: here we attribute the unnatural to some kind of supernatural setting, for exmample heaven or hell (think of the god game, Black and White, where players have godlike powers over characters and are infiltrated by voices of good (an angelic character) and evil (a demonic guide).

8. Invitation to "free play", where mutually contradictory storylines, or endings, are seen as an invitation to create one's own story, which is a common feature of hypertext fiction, but we may well ask other players what their preferred ending of The Stanley Parable is, since we're dealing with a game that thematises non-closure, multi-linearity, logical contradiction and cyclicality.

And yet we may just as well adopt an unnaturalising reading strategy (Nielsen 2013), in an attempt to accept the impossible as it is without trying to make sense of it. This approach goes

against "domesticating the unnatural" (Alber 2013a), and can be
described in terms of a "Zen way of reading" (Alber 2013c, 83–84).
We adopt the stoic position of simply leaving things unexplained
and accepting the feeling of confusion, frustration, or discomfort
that the narrative experience may evoke in us.

Video Games as Unnatural Narratives

Having covered a lot of theory, let's now turn to videogames as
unnatural narratives. I was wondered, while writing, whether I
should put a question mark on the title this essay, but I think it is
fair to claim that in many ways games are unnatural narratives
par excellence. Having said that, this proposition only holds true if
we adopt a broad concept of unnaturalness as, for example, put
forward by Alber (2013a), who defines it as that which is physically
or logically impossible when measured against the foil of our
real-world cognitive frames. In actual fact, we may go as far to
say that under this definition the unnaturalness of games is what
makes them so attractive to vast amounts of people around the
world. The unnaturalness of games enables us to escape into
realms of what's normally thought to be humanly impossible or
unthinkable. Furthermore, we have to bear in mind that games
are perhaps the most readily "naturalising" media of all because
they integrate in their procedural mechanics the very structures
(unnatural or not) and "ecological" interactions (Linderoth 2011).
Players are meant to internalise these structures and interactions
as effectively as possible for fast progress through the game and
to achieve high levels of satisfaction during play.

Clearly, mainstream videogames are full of *physical* impossibilities. These are just a few examples:
- Respawning and rebirth are crucial replayability factors
  (violating the truth condition of singular mortality).
- Games thrive on using fantasy traditions from other
  media such as talking animals, monsters and other forms
  of non-human yet anthropomorphised creatures.

- Human or not, the anatomic dimensions of some hyper-sexualised characters would be anatomically impossible in the real world (think of the early Lara Croft's athletic abilities vis-à-vis her hyper-feminised physique).
- Warping, or teleporting, between geographic areas is a standard form of fast in-game movement (violating the limitations of physical movement).
- Similarly, there are highly dexterous types of movement in some games that are more akin to those of animals than human beings (think of the wall runs in Prince of Persia (1989), the jumping art of SuperMario (1985) and other platform characters, the superhumanly fast-paced balancing act of Mirror's Edge and quite generally the fact that falling or jumping off high edges often doesn't result in character death or even the slightest degree of harm).
- Multiple impersonations of one and the same player are a key attraction of role playing games (RPGs) and MMOGs: either synchronously (with more than one avatar of the same player in a game world simultaneously) or asynchronously (anatomically shape-shifting avatars through customisation).

But games also exhibit a range of conventionalised *logical* impossibilities:

- The fact that avatars are "us" in the game world makes them the interactional metaleptic tool par excellence (Ryan 2004b), yet metalepsis (in the sense of transgressing ontological boundaries, and especially those of fictional and actual worlds) is both physically and logically impossible because we can't all of a sudden lose our anatomic materiality; nor can we be in two places at the same time, especially if they're in different time zones.
- The success of a lot of games is based on the fact that they offer multiple and either contradictory or incompatible endings. Dragon Age: Origins (2009), for example, converges (despite seemingly countless choices throughout)

to four endings (which is a comparably low number, incidentally). Each ending sees different characters ruling the game world, and some characters either dead or alive (which is a logical incompatibility).

So does all this mean that we should stop here and simply conclude that unnatural narratology doesn't work with games because "video games as unnatural narratives" is a tautology? To me this would be slightly myopic because, clearly, when we look at Richardson's anti-mimetically oriented conceptualisation and move beyond the conventionalised "unnatural" media-specificity of games, there's actually quite a lot we can do with a specific type of game: games that seek to defamiliarise and innovate the gaming experience through highly idiosyncratic ludo-narrative mechanics.

So in a second move I would argue that some games are more "unnatural" (in a Richardsonian sense of aesthetically "more estranging") than others because they deliberately violate the ludo-narrative conventions of their genre and the medium itself in order to evoke meta-ludic and meta-fictional reflections in the player – as well as other types of philosophical and critical processes. With this premise in mind, I shall now move on to the analytical part of this essay and demonstrate three aspects of unnaturalness at play: unnatural spatiality in *The Path*, unnatural temporality in *Braid* and unnatural narration in *The Stanley Parable*.

Unnatural Spatiality in *The Path*

According to Alber (2013a), "impossible spaces undo our assumptions about space and spatial organization in the real world". So typical types of unnatural spaces include:
- containers that are bigger on the outside than on the inside, or vice versa
- shape-shifting settings
- non-actualisable geographies

- visions of the infinite and unimaginable universe
- metaleptic jumps between different ontological spheres.

What interests me most here is how the impossible, in the sense of anti-mimetic spatial design, contributes to reflexivity, and one game where this can be shown quite nicely is Tale of Tales's *The Path*.

The Path is a short horror game in which the adolescent female characters we can choose to play are exposed to different types of trauma – tailored to their age. The game world and our inter-action with it is designed in such a way as to evoke horror and premonitions of what may happen. Such contemplative affects are partly created through slow movement through the game world (it's impossible to run for more than a few seconds and the forest of the game world seems endless, which is augmented by a wrap-around structure that causes the player to move in cir-cles). Whenever a girl meets her wolf (and experienced spiritual death as a result), she ends up lying in front of her grandmother's house, which on the outside looks fairly small. As she enters the house, however, it becomes gigantic, and the semi-cut-scene after her "fall" takes us through seemingly endless corridors with countless doors and huge rooms displaying objects evocative of her nightmarish experience. So the logically impossible spatial dimensions of the house (the incompatibility between out-side and inside) can be read in terms of Alber's subjectification strategy (the attribution of unnaturalness to internal states; trauma in this case).[13]

Another interesting element of unnatural spatiality is the treat-ment of paratext vis-à-vis the game world: the girls' journals, retrievable from the game's official website, read very much like they've been written by the fictional characters. However, numerous real-world comments have been posted by players

---

13   Another way of understanding this spatial incompatibility would be in terms of positing a transcendental realm (Alber 2013c) – that of some kind of highly unsettling afterlife.

of the game, which are interspersed with pre-scripted posts by
fictional characters, creating an ontological blurring between
the player's actual world and the fictional world of the game. In
fact, this occurrence of interactional metalepsis (or transgression
between logically distinct ontological spheres) adds to the eerie
but also philosophical and reflective atmosphere of the game. We
accept the unnaturalness of this design feature because we can
read the game as an allegory (one of Alber's (2013b) strategies) of
the trials and tribulations of young women, and this allows our
actual world and the game world to converge.

Unnatural Temporality in *Braid*

My second analysis focuses on unnatural temporality. In an essay
on temporal paradoxes in narrative, Ryan (2009, 142) proposes
four core intuitive human beliefs about time:
1. Time flows, and it does so in a fixed direction.
2. You cannot fight this flow and go back in time.
3. Causes always precede their effects.
4. The past is written once for all.

In fiction, of course, at least some of these dictums are regularly
subverted, for example, in time-travel narratives or postmodern,
multi-linear, filmic narratives such as *Groundhog Day* (1993) or
Run Lola Run (1998). Hence, some elements of (fictional) unnatural
temporality have already been conventionalised depending
on individual levels of exposure and culture-specific media
ecologies.

According to Alber (and his broad definition of unnaturalness),
"unnatural temporalities [which revolve around Ryan's principles]
challenge our real-world ideas about time and temporal progression" (2013a). So for this study we need to add the assumption of
anti-mimetic defamiliarisation as part of the developer's intent.

Typical unnatural temporalities (Richardson 2002) include:

- retrogressive/antinomic temporality, where the scripts of everyday life are reversed (for example, in Martin Amis's 1991 novel Time's Arrow)
- eternal temporal loops/circular temporalities, where the narrative, or a character, seems to be going round in circles (a common feature of hypertext fiction)
- conflated time lines (or "chronomontages"), which conjoin different temporal zones, such as the time traveller landing in the historical past (for example, Kevin from Time Bandits (Gilliam 1981), catapulted into Ancient Greece, in his own contemporary clothes, taking photos with his Polaroid camera)
- reversed causalities, where the present is caused by the future, like in D. M. Thomas's The White Hotel (1981) where the protagonist's pain is caused by an anticipatory projection of a future event
- contradictory temporalities, in which there are mutually exclusive events or sequences, for example, in Coover's 1969 short story "The Babysitter", where Mr. Tucker both did and did not go home to have sex with the babysitter
- differential time lines, such as different aging speeds between characters like in Virginia Woolf's Orlando (1928)
- multiple time lines, plotlines that begin and end at the same time yet take different periods of time to unfold, for example, in Shakespeare's A Midsummer Night's Dream (c1590).

A game that embeds a number of unnatural temporalities quite firmly and unavoidably in its mechanics is Jonathan Blow's *Braid*. It's a 2D platform game where the protagonist, Tim, is on a quest to save the Princess, beg her forgiveness and live happily ever after (although we later learn that she doesn't actually want him). The game as a whole can be read as an allegory of the Trinity nuclear bomb test of 1945, which directly preceded the destruction of Hiroshima and Nagasaki.

Hence, against this backdrop, the impossible temporal mechanics of the game can meaningfully be read as an allegory (see Alber's reading strategies) of the irreversibility of human action and suffering, while the mechanics seem to suggest that the rules of temporal logic can be lifted by Faustian ambitions.

Each world in *Braid* has its own impossible temporal mechanics, which have to be internalised by players (against their real-world and genre-specific assumptions) in order to be successful. I'll only mention three examples here:

- Retrogressive temporality. You can go back in time in exact reversed order by holding the shift key (and speed up the time as needed); hence Tim can "un-die" (rather than res-pawn) indefinitely, and indeed certain achievements only become possible through this rewind function.
- Reversed causality (which goes against the principle that causes always precede their effects). In world three (Time and Mystery), the player's actions can be rewound whilst other elements in the game world remain unaffected by the reversal. For example, using the rewind function, a key can be brought back to the immediate past (without losing the key) to open a door that otherwise wouldn't be possible to open because Tim would be stuck forever in a pit that he's jumped into to grab the key.
- Differential timelines. In world six (Hesitance), the player can slow down time to get certain things done – time moves slower in the proximity of the all-important ring, marked with a halo, enabling Tim to, for example, escape certain monsters while either he or they are in a time warp, or to manipulate the velocity of moving objects, such as clouds, to facilitate forward movement.

Unnatural Narration in *The Stanley Parable*

Finally, I'd like to examine an instance of unnatural narration. Again, unnatural narration can quite simply be any physically impossible narrator (according to Alber), such as an animal, a baby, a human bodily organ, a plant or object. Or it can, and in my mind more powerfully so, manifest itself in unconventionalised forms of extreme narration, such as second-person narration, multiperson narration, certain forms of unreliable narration and de-narration (a narrator's negation of previously stated or assumed truths; see Richardson (2006) for a comprehensive overview). Strangely or not, omniscient, or authorial narration is also generally held to be unnatural, largely because no-one can possibly know as much as a standard omniscient narrator tends to, and the fascination associated with this paradox is reflected in recent fictional creativity beyond print, as my example will show.

What's important to note here is that unnatural narration in games is in itself tautological. A narrator, or narrative voice telling the story, is impossible in videogames because it would subvert or hinder the player's decision-making process in the game world, as well as their individualised emergent experiences.

The game I'm going to look at, *The Stanley Parable* by Davey Wreden/Galactic Café (the remake version of 2013), experiments with this paradox by employing an intriguing type of unnatural narration – a shape-shifting, intrusive narrator whose would-be omniscience is deconstructed by the player's subversive behaviour. The game stages combat between player and narrator. The narrator, as it turns out, isn't as empowered and omniscient as he pretends to be, and is ultimately at the mercy of the player and, of course, the essence of the gameplay and its impact on the narrative design. By the same token, we as players are confronted with the limitations of our own agency as even the choices we can make are pre-scripted.

At this juncture, let me say a few words about omniscient narration. It was the standard form of realistic storytelling in nineteenth-century realism, was then superseded by reflector mode and internal narrative styles in literary modernism (for example James Joyce and Virginia Wolf) and has more recently, in twenty-first-century fiction, seen a revival, yet in very different forms that reflect the impossibility of godlike or representative knowledge or insight. Writers such as Zadie Smith, Salman Rushdie and Martin Amis have been experimenting with more vulnerable, fragmented, confessional forms of authorial narration that reflect both a crisis of fiction writing and, at the same time, the ambition to create new forms of literary authority and thereby regain cultural capital vis-à-vis popular culture (Dawson 2013). So if, in *The Stanley Parable*, we are confronted with an experimental battle between would-be omniscient narrator and player-character, we have to see this design as a reflection of two current trends: (a) the media-ecological crisis and cultural ambitions of twenty-first-century fiction writing, and: (b) the literary gaming movement that's been evolving over the past 15 years or so.

According to its official site, *The Stanley Parable* is "an exploration of story, games, and choice. Except the story doesn't matter, it might not even be a game, and if you ever actually do have a choice, well let me know how you did it" (Mularcyzk, n.d.). So what the game tries to get across is the question of how much agency and choice players actually have in a game and that agency is ultimately illusory (MacCallum-Stewart and Parsler 2007) given that choices, paths and endings tend to be pre-coded. We also learn through procedural rhetoric that subversiveness on the part of the player is a *sine qua non* to escape from illusory agency, which makes cheating not simply a legitimate but indeed a recommended form of player engagement.

The protagonist is Stanley, an office worker in a Kafkaesque corporate, bureaucratic environment, who pushes buttons upon command, day-in, day-out. Initially Stanley, played in the first-person, sets out on his quest to find out what's happened to his co-workers, who have all disappeared. The narrator accompanies him on his way throughout, giving instructions as to where to go next yet not in a directive, command form, but in the past tense indicative, thereby making propositions about what Stanley *did* (before he gets a chance to do so) rather than suggestions about where he *might* go. Whereas in a film or print narrative, past tense indicative narration is the accepted, default standard of storytelling, in a game it completely goes against the grain and seems patronising at best. This makes us, as players, suspicious about the reliability or trustworthiness of the narrator right from the outset, and the more we attempt to deviate from the narrator's propositions, the more stand-offish and annoyed he becomes, so much so that in some extremely deviant endings his comments, behaviour and designs suggest frustration, despair, resignation, or even madness.

The narrator (or implied author) becomes our main enemy in the game because there aren't really any further major obstacles or enemies to overcome. This battle between implied author (man-ifested in the choices built into the game) and the player who strives to undermine his or her "implied" counterpart (personified by the conformist, Stanley) is orchestrated in at least 18 different paths or endings.

In what follows, I'm going to briefly look at three of them to dem-onstrate the transformation of the narrator's projected authority. First, the life ending, which follows the path of maximum con-formism and obedience; secondly, the choice, or real person ending, where you unplug a phone that you were supposed to answer; and thirdly, the museum ending, which adds another ontological sphere, or diegetic level, to the game world, lifting the story experienced so far onto a symbolic or allegorical plane.

The main decision players have to make for Stanley is at a set of two doors, where the "correct" path is left and the "deviant" path is right (paradoxically or not). Stanley can still "go wrong" after taking the "right" door, and very drastically so, going by the narrator's perplexed reactions. If the player follows all the narrator's propositions precisely, in the life ending, they'll be rewarded with a "win". Stanley switches off the controls in the Orwellian Mind Control Facility and steps out into the open.

However, this is not the point of this game, which is indicated two-fold: by the ensuing cut-scene, which leaves the player passively watching and listening to the narrator's freedom monologue on Stanley's alleged "happiness"; and by the fact that, after the cut-scene the player is sent straight back to the beginning, that is, to Stanley's office, with the interspersed loading message "the end is never the end", suggesting that they're supposed to explore the paths of deviance or defiance.

Fig. 1 shows the diegetic levels of the game world as evoked by the life ending. The big box contains the diegetic, or fictional space of the game, with the intradiegetic, or character level embedded in the narrator's diegesis. We as players are extradiegetic or outside the story, but since we implement the narrator's story, which he tells to a narratee on his level, by steering Stanley, we're also inevitably part of the game world. Therefore the membranes between the levels, or spheres, are shown as semi-permeable: we can see that there are a lot of metaleptic cross-overs happening already, even though the narrator isn't actually addressing us directly (which he does in other endings).

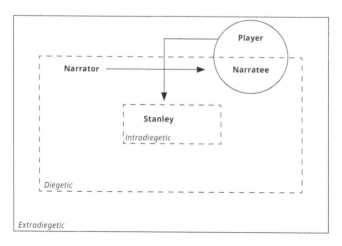

Fig. 1: Diegetic levels of The Stanley Parable life ending.

A striking example of the narrator's reaction to player deviance is the choice, or real person ending. Here the player opts to unplug a phone that Stanley was supposed to answer, thereby undertaking an action not contained within the narrator's script. This act of transgression causes the narrator to sense that there's someone else behind Stanley's incorrect behaviour, and after first addressing Stanley and realising Stanley couldn't possibly have devised such an act, he turns to the implied player thus:

> Oh no, no, no! Did you just unplug the phone? That wasn't supposed to be a choice. How did you do that? You actually chose incorrectly, but I didn't even know that was possible. Let me double-check *[shuffling his papers around yet finding no evidence of this choice in his script]* … I don't understand. How on earth are you making meaningful choices? What did you … Wait a second … How had I not noticed it sooner? You're not Stanley. You're a real person. I can't believe I was so mistaken. This is why you've been able to make correct and incorrect choices, and to think I've been letting you run around in this game for so long! If you'd made any more wrong choices you might have negated it entirely. It's as though you'd completely ignored even the most basic safety protocol for real-world decision-making. I'm going to stop the game for a moment so we can educate you properly on safe decision making.

This is followed by a satirical educational video about the life-threatening potential of human decision-making. So in this instance the narrator breaks the fourth wall and moves the metaleptic interaction onto an (implied) extra-diegetic level. Another observation that can be made here is that this particular ending shows how indirect communication works between the developer and the player outside the fictional world (extra-diegetically; marked by the dotted arrow in Fig. 2), as we learn that the narrator is not responsible for the phone that can be unplugged as a pre-programmed choice. So here the actual author

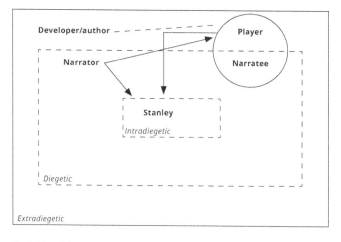

Fig. 2: Diegetic levels as suggested by the Choice Ending.

communicates implicitly with the actual player, who implements the communicated option intra-diegetically.

Interestingly, as the camera returns to the game world and the room with the telephone, we find the space transformed into a postmodern pastiche (Fig. 4), and the narrator says, "Ah welcome back! You may have noticed that this room has begun to deteriorate as a result of narrative contradiction" and, "We just need to get you home as soon as possible before the narrative contradiction gets any worse. Unfortunately it seems this place is not well equipped to deal with reality". So here the narrator himself explicates the anti-mimetic, logical impossibilities embedded in the game's narrative design.

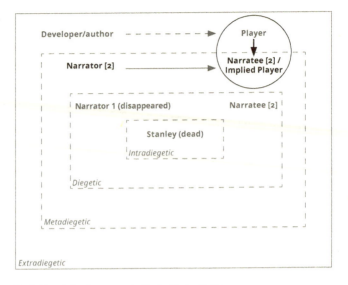

Fig. 3: Diegetic levels as suggested by the Choice Ending.

Finally, in the museum ending, Stanley meets his intra-diegetic death after choosing to take the escape route, branching off the "correct" track to the Mind Control Facility. He's killed by some kind of machine, yet again we find that the game goes on and the player (now playing their own alter ego) finds him or herself in a fictional developer's museum, which exhibits all sorts of in-game props and concept art. Strikingly, here we encounter another narrator, a female voice, which seems to be superordinate to the diegesis of the initial male narrator, who now seems to have disappeared along with Stanley. The female narrator comments on the paradoxical love-hate relationship between player-character and narrator and advises the player to stop the game to put an end to the endless, meaningless cycle of "walking someone else's path". And here, finally, is where the player's alter ego in the game dies, crushed by the "metal jaws". After this ending players have

Fig. 4: Postmodern telephone room in the choice ending.

to physically reload the game by starting again from the main menu.

In Fig. 4 we can see that another level of diegesis, call it meta-diegesis, has been added to the ontological universe of the game, and the female narrator speaks to us directly as implied players. Interestingly, though, although the female super-narrator seems to be more empowered than the male narrator in the other endings, she is equally subject to the player's choices (and of course the game design). She frantically tries to prevent the player from having his or her alter ego killed in the game world, and from endlessly perpetuating the cycle of following pre-designed paths and subjection to illusory agency.

To wrap up this analysis, *The Stanley Parable*'s procedural rhetoric reinforces the decoding strategy suggested by its title (a parable is an educational allegory). As players we are made to read it as an allegory of illusory agency built into games to give players the illusion of choice, power and control. In fact, we as players are all

Stanley because again and again we willingly or even enthusiastically subject ourselves to the constraints set by the games we play, except of course when we cheat – and this is where we have the power to "defeat" the implied author-programmer.

Concluding Remarks

To sum up the main insights I've drawn from this research so far, if we want to move toward an unnatural ludo-narratology, there are several things to be aware of and take into account. First, not every definition of unnaturalness is useful for close game analysis, but if we take anti-mimeticism and defamiliarisation – for the sake of entertainment, flow, innovation and critical reflection – as a starting point, we can begin to make sense of the kinds of "unnatural structures" that feature, for example, in meta-games like *The Stanley Parable*, or generally in games that push the boundaries of ludo-narrative design.

Second, the "naturalising" and "unnaturalising" reading strategies put forward by Alber (2013b) and Nielsen (2013) are useful starting points, yet they have to be augmented by game-specific ways of making sense of what Jesper Juul (2005, 132) calls "incoherent worlds", that is, by explaining unnaturalness in terms of the rules of the game. Furthermore, there's still a lot of work to be done on studying players' individual nuances in understanding unnatural ludo-narrative structures and their underlying and resulting play styles and strategies. Closer insights into these processes can only be gained through empirical player research.

Finally, I'd propose an inductive approach to developing a medium-specific toolkit for unnatural ludo-narrative structures, taking into account the multiple ways in which game mechanics allow us to execute procedural rhetoric to "read" design features, such as illusory agency, slow gaming, action reversal and character duplication, functionally and with a view to gaining a deeper understanding of videogames as a narrative art.

Acknowledgements: *I would like to thank a number of people whose comments on earlier drafts of this essay paper have been invaluable: Jan Alber, Anne Dippel, Sonia Fizek, Jesper Juul, Matti Karhulati, Niklas Schrape, and Annika Waern.*

Bibliography

Alber, Jan. 2013a. "Unnatural Narrative". In *The Living Handbook of Narratology*, edited by Peter Hühn et al. Hamburg: Hamburg University. Accessed June 23, 2015: http://www.lhn.uni-hamburg.de/article/unnatural-narrative.

Alber, Jan. 2013b. "Unnatural Narratology: The Systematic Study of Anti-Mimeticism". *Literature Compass* 10 (5): 449–60.

Alber, Jan. 2013c. "Unnatural Spaces and Narrative Worlds". In *A Poetics of Unnatural Narrative*, edited by Jan Alber, Henrik Skov Nielsen, and Brian Richardson, 45–66. Columbus: Ohio State University Press.

Alber, Jan, Stefan Iversen, Henrik Skov Nielsen, and Brian Richardson. 2010. "Unnatural Narratives, Unnatural Narratology: Beyond Mimetic Models." *Narrative* 18 (2): 113–36.

Alber, Jan and Rüdiger Heinze, eds. 2011. *Unnatural Narratives – Unnatural Narratology*. Berlin: De Gruyter.

Culler, Jonathan. 1975. *Structuralist Poetics: Structuralism, Linguistics and the Study of Literature*. London: Routledge.

Dawson, Paul. 2013. *The Return of the Omniscient Narrator: Authorship in Twenty-First Century Fiction*. Columbus: Ohio State University Press.

Ensslin, Astrid. 2011. *The Language of Gaming*. Basingstoke: Palgrave Macmillan.

Ensslin, Astrid. 2014. *Literary Gaming*. Cambridge: MIT Press.

Ensslin, Astrid, and Alice Bell. Forthcoming. *Unnatural Narratives and Digital Fiction*. Invited for review by Ohio State University Press.

Fludernik, Monika. 1996. *Towards a "Natural" Narratology*. London: Routledge.

Hayles, N. Katherine. 2007. "Hyper and Deep Attention: The Generational Divide in Cognitive Modes". *Profession* 13: 187–99.

Heinze, Anna, Albert Schirrmeister, and Julia Weitbrecht, eds. 2013. *Antikes Erzählen. Narrative Transformationen von Antike in Mittelalter und Früher Neuzeit.* Transformationen der Antike 27. Berlin: De Gruyter.

Herman, David. 1999. *Narratologies: New Perspectives on Narrative Analysis*. Columbus: Ohio State University Press.

Jenkins, Henry. 2004. "Game design as narrative architecture". In *First Person: New Media as Story, Performance, and Game*, edited by Noah Wardrip-Fruin, and Pat Harrigan (eds), 118–30. Cambridge, MA: MIT Press.

Jenkins, Henry. 2006. *Convergence Culture: Where Old and New Media Collide*. New York: New York University Press.

Juul, Jesper. 2005. *Half-Real: Video Games Between Real Rules and Fictional Worlds*. Cambridge, MA: MIT Press.

Linderoth, Jonas. 2011. "Beyond the Digital Divide: An Ecological Approach to
Gameplay". *Proceedings of DiGRA 2011 (September 14–17)*. Utrecht School of the
Arts. Accessed May 20, 2015. http://www.digra.org/wp-content/uploads/digital-
library/11307.03263.pdf.

McCallum-Stewart, Esther, and Justin Parsler. 2007. "Illusory Agency in Vampire: The
Masquerade – Bloodlines" *dichtung-digital* 37. Accessed January 11, 2013. http://
dichtung-digital.de/2007/maccallumstewart_parsler.htm.

Mularcyzk, Sam (n.d.) "The Stanley Parable: A Galactic Café Game". Accessed May
29, 2015. http://www.stanleyparable.com.

Nielsen, Henrik Sklov. 2013. "Naturalizing and Unnaturalizing Reading Strategies."
In *A Poetics of Unnatural Narrative*, edited by Jan Alber, Henrik Skov Nielsen, and
Brian Richardson, 67–93. Columbus: Ohio State University Press.

Richardson, Brian. 2002. "Beyond Story and Discourse: Narrative Time in Post-
modern and Nonmimetic Fiction". In *Narrative Dynamics: Essays on Time, Plot,
Closure, and Frames*, edited by Brian Richardson, 47–63. Columbus: Ohio State
University Press.

Richardson, Brian. 2006. *Unnatural Voices: Extreme Narration in Modern and Contemporary Fiction*. Columbus: Ohio State University Press.

Richardson, Brian. 2011. "What is Unnatural Narrative Theory?". In *Narrative –
Unnatural Narratology*, edited by Jan Alber and Rüdiger Heinze, 23–40. Berlin: de
Gruyter.

Richardson, Brian. 2015. *Unnatural Narrative: Theory, History, and Practice*. Columbus:
Ohio State University Press.

Ryan, Marie-Laure. 2004a. *Narrative Across Media*. Lincoln: University of Nebraska
Press.

Ryan, Marie-Laure. 2004b. "Metaleptic Machines". *Semiotica* 150 (1): 439–69.

Ryan, Marie-Laure. 2009. "Temporal Paradoxes in Narrative". *Style* 43 (2): 142–64.

Šklovskij, Viktor. 1965. "Art as Technique". *Russian Formalist Criticism*, edited by Lee T.
Leemon and Marion J. Reis, 3–24. Lincoln: University of Nebraska Press.

Ludography

Black and White (2001). Electronic Arts.

Braid (2009). USA: Number None, Inc. Jonathan Blow.

Dragon Age: Origins (2009). Electronic Arts.

Everquest (1999). Sony Online Entertainment

Mirror's Edge (2008). Rhianna Pratchett. Electronic Arts.

Prince of Persia (1989). Jordan Mechner. Brøderbund.

Progress Quest (2002). Eric Fredricksen.

Red Dead Redemption (2010). Rockstar San Diego. Rockstar Games.

SuperMario (1985). Shigeru Miyamoto. Nintendo.

The Stanley Parable (2013). Galactic Café/Davey Wreden.

Is Hacking the Brain the Future of Gaming?

An interview with Karen Palmer

Among the four keynote speakers at DiGRA2015 was digital artist and film maker Karen Palmer. On May 16, in her talk "Is Hacking the Brain the Future of Gaming?", she presented the neurogame SYNCSELF 2 in which the player's thoughts are read and transferred onto an avatar. In a short interview, she explains what the "diversity of play" means to her and talks about the aesthetic potential of combining film and games.

Question: You have developed, and are about to develop, new and innovative formats that combine film with performance, parkour running, and games. Your performance/game *SYNCSELF 2* is an interactive movie that can be performed or navigated by electric signals retrieved from the brain of the player or "interactor". Whenever the interactor focuses and is not distracted by the visuals of the film, the audience, or by his or her diverting thoughts, the characters of the film succeed in their attempt to overcome parkour hurdles. When the interactor loses focus, the characters of the film fail. Is this a film you directed or is it a game you designed?

Karen Palmer: It is both: interactive film and a game. You watch the film and you play the game.

Q: It seems fair to say that it is not only the content of your projects, but also the media you embed your pieces within, are highly diverse. The title of DiGRA2015 was "Diversity of Play: Games – Cultures – Identities". What does "diversity of play" actually mean for you?

KP: Diversity of play means playing in many different formats and genres to create an innovative audience journey through a gaming experience.

Q: How did your personal journey arrive at the crossroads of parkour and interactive film?

KP: In 2009 I became a committed forerunner and, inspired by my passion for parkour, I was encouraged to "move through fear", not just while training but within my life. I left the security of a successful career as a creative director and music video director to pursue my passion to be a visual artist and develop my voice as a storyteller.

As a result, I have developed my own unique interactive transmedia experiences that innovatively fuse well-being with art, film, parkour and gaming experiences through tech and storytelling to create an experience where the user is the remote control and the action is completely dependent on the psychological state of the user. My objective is to inspire and empower the user through storytelling.

Q: Much of your work is located at the intersection of visual art, interactive film and gaming. How would you describe the (aesthetic) potentials of combining film and games?

KP: The aesthetic potentials of combining film and gaming offer an exciting opportunity to create a fully immersive cinematic experience.

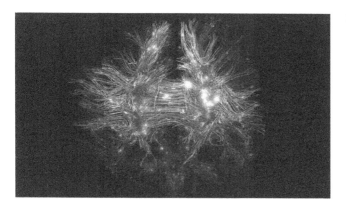

Transforming film from a purely linear journey, of which the director is the sole author, into a journey with multiple potential story structures of which the audience is the controller of the experience. This approach creates a bespoke, personalised and highly satisfying journey for the viewer/ player.

Unlike animation, film is a more visual reality-based gaming experience so the type of immersion into this world possess a different set of dynamics and therefore has the potential to be a more powerful journey.

Q: *SYNCSELF 2*, to name one of your last projects, combines "neurogaming" with film. What exactly does the term mean and how do neurogaming techniques transform the gaming experience?

KP: Neurogaming is where your mind and body meet game play. It is about integrating one's full nervous system into the gaming experience for the purposes of entertainment, health, education, wellness and more.

Neurogame developers are using the latest emotional, cognitive, sensory and behavioural technologies to create radically compelling experiences to engage and entertain gamers worldwide.

Q: From your point of view, what are the risks and opportunities of the more and more blurred distinctions between games and non-games?

KP: I am not aware of any potential risks, however, I see a lot of potential opportunities. New forms of learning and self-development through an engaging format. The experience enables the user to develop self, and gain practical cognitive skills such as focus, enabling the user to become more productive through a training experience. Acquiring real world skills through this unique form of "entertainment-meets-gaming" will enable the user to understand their strengths and weakness better.

There are quite a few examples of pieces that build upon interactive gaming experiences. To mention just a few, recent developments include:

SYNCSELF 2 created an environment for the user where they are able to explore the concept of self. The user then became aware of process of focus. As a result they were then able to access it at will.

SuperBetter is another application that helps you achieve your health goals — or recover from an illness or injury — by increasing your personal resilience. Resilience means staying curious, optimistic and motivated even in the face of the toughest challenges.

Q: Karen, could you please give one more example here?

KP: *Nevermind* is a biofeedback-enhanced adventure horror game that takes you into the dark and twisted world of the subconscious.

As you explore surreal labyrinths and solve the puzzles of the mind, a biofeedback sensor will monitor how scared or

stressed you become moment-to-moment. If you let your fears get the best of you, the game will become harder. If you're able to calm yourself in the face of terror, the game will be more forgiving.

Nevermind strives to create a haunting gameplay experience that also teaches you how to be more aware of your internal responses to stressful situations. If you can learn to control your anxiety within the disturbing realm of *Nevermind*, just imagine what you can do when it comes to those inevitable stressful moments in the real world ...

Q: In science fiction, plugging into the brain has often quite evil connotations. I can see from your artwork that the actors/runners/players look quite happy with what you do with them, but could you imagine ethical problems with neurogaming?

KP: Neurogaming is where the mind and body meet game play. It's where your full nervous system is integrated into the gaming experience by using new sensor technologies, output systems, and game design techniques.

I do not envisage any ethical issues at this time, as it is merely another form of evaluating data, which is becoming all the more pervasive in society.

Q: Can you give us a description of your forthcoming piece *FUTURESELF*?

KP: *FUTURESELF* will build upon the success of *SYNCSELF 2* and has the potential to create an even more significant impact culturally through a more precise user experience. *FUTURESELF* will build upon this functionality to measure the vibrational frequency that we as humans transmit.

Q: Karen, what is "vibrational frequency"? Can you please explain in a few sentences?

KP: *FUTURESELF* will monitor the vibrational, emotional, and mental frequency that the user is operating at and, through the immersive storytelling experience, be guided to raise their vibrational level. The process of interacting with the installation will improve the user's sense of awareness and increase their sense of mindfulness enabling them to become their "future self" through the experience. The functionality will be both a solo and multi-player experience, where two players are able to compete to become their "future self".

Q: *Thank you very much for the interview.*

Navigating Uncertainty: Ludic Epistemology in an Age of New Essentialisms

Markus Rautzenberg

Like for Freud, psychoanalysis for Lacan was always more than just a catalogue of curing methods for illnesses of the mind but also about human existence as a whole. In his famous talk at the Catholic University of Louvain, that was in part published in the TV documentary *Jacques Lacan parle* (1972), one of his claims is as simple as it is radical: he suggests that there is no such thing as certainty, not even in death.

But what does this really mean? Isn't death (and taxes one might add) the only entity in life that is unavoidable? Isn't it absurd to propose that we can't be sure of death? What he means, of course, is that it is certain that we will die but that we live *as if* that was not the case. Not because we decide to do so, or because of some narcissistic hubris, but because the certainty of death is, in itself, a belief and a system of faith because our psychological system cannot empirically experience its own annihilation. Sure, we see people (fictional and real) die almost every day in the media and, depending on our profession or as soon as we reach a certain age, it also becomes part of our personal life.

However, in our subconscious "heart of hearts", we don't know death, or to be more precise, we don't know *our own death*.

Death is a barrier for our psyche that we cannot overcome. In an abstract way we know that we must die of course, but we don't know it in an actual way in the same sense that we know what it is like to be hungry or how it feels to be tired for example. Our own death is something that is, in an existential sense, not knowable, because it is a mode of existence, that – obviously – cannot be experienced as such.

Lacan proposes that instead of experiencing death there is simply a belief that death exists and that we don't live for all eternity. The function of this belief, it's structuring mechanism, is as paradoxical as it may sound: hope and consolation. Hope in the finitude of suffering, of futility or absurdity. Consolation in the fact that one day whatever is currently happening to us as an individual or as a species will come to an end.

To sum it up: according to Lacan our relationship to death is actually the opposite of what we normally believe. One of our most intimate and crushing states of existential fear (when, for example, we wake up at night with the thought "I am going to die" appearing suddenly out of nowhere), is not intimate or per-sonal at all. It is a structuring system of faith, a concept, coming from the outside, whose purpose is not to frighten us, but on the contrary, to make life bearable. *The problem is not that there is death but that deep down we assume that we are immortal.* And this delusion is what is really destructive. Without it, nobody would smoke or take drugs (or wage wars for that matter). But without it, we probably wouldn't be human. Consequently, it is not the fear of death that is specific to us as a species, it is our delusion of immortality.

It is easy to see that these two notions – the delusion of immortality on the one hand and, on the other, death as a belief system to keep the latter in check – are in conflict. So what is the purpose of explaining all this? The point is that *uncertainty*

is absolute, as paradoxical as that may be; that the one thing in
the world we think we can take for granted is, at least for our
psychological reality, not certain at all. Death (and life for that
matter) are concepts that structure the psyche from the outside, that we assume and internalise like other famous Lacanian
categories such as the imaginary and the symbolic, because
death belongs to the realm of the real; it is the outer limit of our
existence.

So we don't know death, we just know *of* it. That means that even
death isn't certain, because what do we really know? Don't we all
get much older nowadays? In the so-called "first-world" countries,
life expectancies are constantly rising and who knows what will
be in 30 or 50 years. As we all know, just a little over one hundred
years ago, you could die from the flu. You could have to work so
hard you could die of exhaustion before the age of 30. Today, to
conceive of death, we must think of it as being caused by rare or
extreme events, like cancer or fatal accidents. Meanwhile trans-
humanism is hard at work to bring us some form of immortality.

This kind of relentless uncertainty that doesn't exclude
death seems to be the condition of contemporary western
societies. Structuralism and especially post-structuralism
were philosophies that embraced this notion and pushed
its theoretical implications to their limits, to a point where
countermeasures where eventually inevitable: countermeasures
that emerged from within post-structuralism itself. The
apocalyptic cultural pessimism of Jean Baudrillard or Paul
Virillo for example, who claimed that we live in an age of total
simulation in which everything real has dissolved into media
technologies, is a logical albeit conservative answer to a world
without transcendental signifiers. The modification in their
theoretical approach was subtle but important: they accepted
the status quo of absolute uncertainty as a given but undermined
the radicalism of the notion with the implication that a world
of meaning and representations of the real has been *lost*. But
having lost something is still better than the idea there was never

anything to lose in the first place. And it is not hard to see why these countermeasures have emerged: how else can we live under conditions of permanent uncertainty?

In this context, new essentialisms have come to the fore with full force (and I am not even talking about Islamism or other kinds of religious or political fundamentalisms). The all-encompassing postmodern uncertainty I just sketched out is demonised as a kind of corrosion or corruption of the spirit, mind and morality. Just take a look at religious fundamentalisms' counterpart: the popular "new atheist" movement and its protagonists, such as Richard Dawkins or the late Christopher Hitchens. Books like *The God Delusion* (Dawkins 2006), or *God is Not Great: How Religion Poisons Everything* by Hitchens (2007), can't hide the fact that in their radical narrow-mindedness they do exactly the same as their declared enemies. They just swap one belief system (in the Lacanian sense) for another, unable to deal with what frightens them most: uncertainty. And to be perfectly clear about it: even though I took Lacan as a starting point, psychoanalysis is, of course, one of the most powerful "belief systems" modernity has ever come up with. There are no privileged perspectives here, just points of departure.

There are aspects of neuroscience and genetics that have become a kind of belief system, not in the sense of an illusion (that is, of course, the punch-line of Lacan's argumentation: "belief systems" are as real and powerful as it gets), but as a *coping mechanism*, protecting us from the insolence of uncertainty. Everyone knows, especially neuroscientists, that colouring areas of brain scans doesn't bring us any closer to understanding the brain, that those pictures are not photographic in nature but algorithm-filtered visualisations, and that the idea of photographic truth is used as persuasive rhetoric to produce evidence where there is none.

In the firm belief that one day the right connections will eventually be made, data-driven research – the sciences' *dernière crie* – analyses the enormous amount of data digital-media are able to provide and treats that data not as an assembly of random occurrences but as a kind of new "book of nature" that is thought to have the potential to someday reveal scientific truth. This is teleological, religious thinking and there is nothing inherently wrong with it as long as one doesn't claim that it is the opposite.

In philosophy and the humanities, non-ontological, post-metaphysical ideas seem to be in a state of decline since the death of Jacques Derrida who, a few years before his death, was accused of "relativism" by none other than Cardinal Ratzinger (the later Pope Benedikt XVI). The accusation was that by claiming that there is no "transcendental signifier", no stable core of truth at the centre of our sign-systems, Derrida and with him the whole of postmodernity, had devalued every religion, political theory and moral system there is, pushing humanity into an intellectually and morally devastating wasteland of "anything goes" that, according to Ratzinger at least, is the blight of modernity.

Today, neo-metaphysical movements in philosophy and the humanities (our obsessions with material culture, speculative realism or our new found love for big holistic theories that try to follow Hegel in their systematic aspirations), may very well be understood someday as expressions of the desire to overcome the constructivisms of the twentieth century and to re-establish a connection with the "real".

And isn't there some truth to this? For example, isn't global capitalism – governed by a fear of uncertainty in the guise of mathematical game theory – showing what it is like when there is nothing certain but uncertainty itself? At its core, economic game theory tries to cope with the old provocation of uncertainty, mathematically this time, exactly like our other "belief systems" let us cope with death. Trying to predict how economic actors behave in relation to other actors is what the algorithms of the global economy are designed for. Since John von Neumann's first paper on the subject this "belief system" has been called *game* theory because it is about *taming uncertainty*, which is what a theory of strategic decision-making is all about.

But this kind of thinking is well-known; it is the rationale of wartime. Trying to domesticate uncertainty at all costs means assuming that we live in a state of constant threat. As we all know, that is the state we live in within a globalised society – a state of *fear*. Fear of the next terrorist attack, fear of losing your job, fear of not being attractive, intelligent or emotionally resilient enough etc. There are many books on the intricacies of the "culture of fear".

It is only a small step from fear to paranoia, and at this point we enter the realm of insanity. It sets in when, in navigating uncertainty, we are tipped off balance, when our belief systems don't work anymore and no longer provide us with the delusion of immortality. Lacan's story about his patient and her *rêve pascalien* exemplifies this. The dream, where existence is infinitely regenerated out of itself ("*l'existence régénérai toujours d'elle même*"), is pure wish fulfilment, piggybacking on the delusion of immortality mentioned before, unleashed from the shackles of the concept of death. What at first glance may seem like an innocent dream appears as a nightmare, leaving the dreamer "half mad" in the process.

What Lacan could only anticipate, however, is that in computer games his Pascalian dream, the insanity of the delusion of immortality, has become an everyday practice made possible by digital media: I am of course referring to the savepoint or, to formulate it closer to Lacans' presentation, the idea of respawning.

The concept behind respawning is one of the most important and defining features of digital media and all the more for computer games in which this kind of time-axis manipulation, as Friedrich Kittler would have called it, is something that no computer game can exist without. The only way to remove this feature would be to design a game that destroys itself after use, deleting its boot directory, or a game that is so short that it doesn't need the feature, like some puzzle games. The Pascalian dream of infinite regeneration has been implemented in many ways and recently quite cleverly in a coming-of-age adventure with the very appropriate title, *Life is Strange* (2015). Here, the hero is an adolescent girl in her first week at a new school. As if this wasn't scary enough, she (and the player) discover they can manipulate time, and not just through the medium of photography – a topic that is regularly reflected upon during the game – but in the diegetic world of the game. Within the game, it opens possibilities teenagers could only dream of. The genius of the game lies in its reflection on the mediality of computer games through two lenses that are also intertwined in the game world: photography and the trials and tribulations of puberty.

Being able to say exactly the right thing at the right time would certainly be a massive boost to a teenagers' fragile self-confidence but this is, of course, still borne out of fear; the fear of uncertainty. Computer games work so well because they provide relief from uncertainty while at the same time work in the very medium of uncertainty itself: games and play (I will elaborate on this shortly). This paradoxical coincidence leads us back to the realm of insanity. From *Planescape Torment (1999)* to *The Suffering (2004)*, from *Manhunt (2003)* to *Eternal Darkness*, from *Sanitarium (1998)* to *Silent Hill (1999) and Heavy Rain (2010), from Psychonauts (2005)* to *Papa y Yo (2012)*, since the very beginning of the medium there has been no end of tales of madness and insanity in computer games. And even in cases where insanity isn't an explicit, central theme of the story, the dystopian worlds and hellish, apocalyptical environments in a game like *World of Warcraft (2004)* can't just point to a juvenile lust for blood and gore.

In computer games we come to somehow *enjoy* insanity. Take, for example, a game like *Bloodborne* (2015), the latest in the infamous series of hardcore roleplaying games the Japanese developer *From Soft* has released since *Demons Souls (2009)*. These games are a nightmare in every sense of the word. Not only is the overall atmosphere of these games meticulously crafted to be as bleak and oppressive as possible, with environments that feel like a Victorian version of a Hieronymus Bosch painting, but the game mechanics are downright punishing. As a game, *Bloodborne* and its brethren are a kind of antithesis to the trend of casual games. Yet at the same time these games are immensely successful. Why? Because in these games, computer games almost come in to their own or "to themselves"; because these games celebrate uncertainty and insanity at the same time, and result in a kind of "gaming bliss" only very few commercial games achieve. At the same time we all know that in a game like this there is no place for real uncertainty, because the design of such a game has to be very tight and every component must fit together, otherwise the result would be so frustrating, that the player wouldn't want to continue. Games like *Bloodborne* are *staging* uncertainty; they revel in it without being able to provide real randomness and entropy, which would be a pre-requisite of true uncertainty.[1]

But, again, in exactly what way are insanity, uncertainty and gaming connected such that the combination makes a hellish nightmare like this so enjoyable? Let's take a hint from Alice because, like always, when in doubt, ask Lewis Carroll!

After venturing through the looking glass, Alice enters a land of paradoxes and permanent metamorphosis. What may look ordinary and normal on first glance always turns into something different, into something unexpected, thus mirroring the experience of a child trying to make sense of the adult world, which, to the child, doesn't make sense at all. It was Gilles Deleuze who famously put together a comprehensive list of these

---

1   Uncertainty as a key component for computer games has recently been re-examined by Greg Costikyan (2013) from the perspective of a game designer, providing many examples of how modes of uncertainty are and can be applied in computer game designs. Early stages of my own, more philosophical approach to the notion of uncertainty in computer games have first been published in: *Spiegelwelt. Elemente einer Aisthetik des Bildschirm-spiels* (Rautzenberg 2002).

paradoxes that haunt not only Alice but the reader as well by implementing them into a theory of meaning (1998). And there is a certain paradox that is the leitmotif of all of Alice's adventures: a certain concurrence of "reality" and "fiction", of actuality and virtuality. This simultaneousness is, of course, embodied by the mirror-twins *Tweedledee* and *Tweedledum* who at one point in *Through the Looking Glass* (Carroll 1912) want to teach Alice about the dreams of the Red King, who is peacefully snoring away under a tree:

> 'He's dreaming now' said Tweedledee: 'and what do you think he is dreaming about?'
>
> Alice said, 'Nobody can guess that.'
>
> 'Why about *you*!' Tweedledee exclaimed, clapping his hands triumphantly. 'And if he left off dreaming about you, where do you suppose you'd be?'
>
> 'Where I am now of course' said Alice.
>
> 'Not you!' Tweedledee retorted contemptuously. 'You'd be nowhere. Why, you're only a sort of thing in his dream!'
>
> 'If that there king was to wake' added Tweedledum, 'you'd go out – bang! – just like a candle!'
>
> 'I shouldn't!' Alice exclaimed indignantly. 'Besides, if I'm only a sort of thing in his dream, what are you, I should like to know?‹'
>
> 'Ditto' said Tweedledum.
>
> 'Ditto, Ditto' cried Tweedledee.
>
> He shouted this so loud that Alice couldn't help saying,

'Hush! You'll be waking him, I'm afraid, if you make so much noise.'[2]

Alice's hesitation is the result of an ontological and epistemological uncertainty. On the one hand she is denying the possibility of her being a non-real "sort of thing" that could vanish like the flame of a candle – "bang!" – if the Red King awakens. On the other hand, however, she would rather not take the risk of waking him, because, in the end, better safe than sorry, right?

At one point during the course of Metal Gear Solid – a game that the Japanese developer Konami released first on Sony's Playstation platform in 1998 – the player in the guise of the avatar and protagonist of the game, Solid Snake,[3] encounters a villain named Psycho Mantis who – according to the in-game mythology – has "telepathic powers". This encounter leads to a boss fight that "proves" the telepathic capabilities of Psycho Mantis in a sophisticated way. If the player has played another game from Konami, for example Castlevania (1986), that has left traces in the form of "save games" on the memory-unit of the console, the game software of Metal Gear Solid is programmed to detect those save games discretely.

The result of this within the game is a baffling display of Mantis's "telepathic powers", because it enables the virtual antagonist to refer directly to behavioral patterns and certain biases of the real player sitting in front of the monitor: "So, you like Castlevania? Ah, you have saved often. You are a prudent person". But Mantis has even more tricks up his sleeve to further substantiate his claims of telepathy: the longer the fight lasts, the more he keeps talking to the player and not to his diegetic opponent. At one point he

2   From Alice's Adventures in Wonderland & Through the Looking Glass (Carroll 2012, 158).

3   The narrative of the game revolves around a global conspiracy that the hero of the game has to stop by infiltrating the headquarters of a secret paramilitary organisation. The villains and protagonists of this virtual play all have codenames that link them to their shared past as parts of a secret governmental task-force called Fox Hound.

demands of the player to lay down his controller, the dual shock pad, on the floor so that Mantis can "take control" of the device. The controller then actually moves on the floor seemingly on its own. A simple trick, because the dual shock pad has two small motors that can cause vibrations inside the device. The trick is simple but effective, because the events "inside" the game seem to reach out into the real world.

The connection between Alice and the user playing the boss fight in *Metal Gear Solid* is obvious: it is the simultaneousness of epistemic, logical and ontological layers that normally cannot coexist on the same plane of existence. Alice's uncertainty regarding her own ontological status is similar to the one that occurs during the encounter with Psycho Mantis in *Metal Gear Solid*. For a short moment the line between dream and reality, virtuality and actuality gets blurred. Most importantly, there is no implicit hierarchy between these different planes; it is unclear which precedes the other. This moment of hesitation and uncertainty, however brief, results for Alice in an irrational fear of being annihilated by the awakening of the King and it is responsible for the bewilderment of the player who observes how a virtual character in a computer game suddenly seems to have power over a real object outside the game, thus being able to reach outside the screen and "beyond the looking glass".

These moments of uncertainty may be brief but their inner dynamics are of great importance. Unlike Alice, Psycho Mantis seems to know that he is part of a fictional, virtual world, therefore the normally impenetrable threshold between fiction and reality seems to crumble. As Psycho Mantis stretches out of the diegetic framing of the computer game as a kind of ludic *trompe l'oeil,* different modes of existence seem to be coexisting that would otherwise be logically, as well as ontologically and epistemically, incompatible. It is the game *as a medium* that makes this possible and it was Gregory Bateson who defined play and games accordingly.

For him one of the most fascinating aspects of game and play is rooted in the very structure that allows for moments of transgression of which the boss fight with Psycho Mantis is of course not the most complex but an effective example. Bateson analyses this aspect of game and play psychologically, utilising the analogy of primary and secondary processes of the psychic system,[4] by developing a theory of game and play as media that are able to transcend these otherwise insurmountable barriers. These moments of transcending define the very mediality of game and play. While the mechanisms of the subconscious primary processes and the discursive secondary processes are normally incompatible with each other, game and play are able to transcend these barriers by mediating the ensuing paradoxes. "It therefore follows that the play frame as here used as an explanatory principle implies a special combination of primary and secondary processes" (Bateson 1972, 191). It is crucial that Bateson analyses game and play as media that are situated between different logical and epistemic layers, mediating between them, without ever synthesising them in a Hegelian-dialectical sense. The paradoxes are not *aufgehoben* but set in motion. *Ludic mediality is a dance of and with paradoxes.*

The dynamics of ludic mediality therefore create a logico-epistemic twilight zone similar to a lucid dream where the dreamer is *suddenly aware* that he or she is dreaming. This specific kind of dream normally occurs within the short liminal space between sleep and awakening. As long as the dreamer is dreaming without being aware of his own state, the dream works within its own operational framing. Not only can the threshold to secondary processes not be transgressed, it cannot even be perceived as such from within the dream. The moment of lucid dreaming, however, suddenly enables the dreamer to draw meta-conclusions, which, according to Bateson, make framings perceivable. This, of course, was the crucial point of entry for

4   Bateson uses Freudian terms here first developed in the *Traumdeutung*.

Erving Goffman's sociological theory of *Frame Analysis*, and from there Bateson's theory of framing helped to theorise second- and third-order observers, which in turn was extremely important for cybernetics, radical constructivism and finally system theory. Therefore, it would be fitting to speak of games as *framed uncertainties*. "Framed" in the sense that Bateson and Goffman suggest and "framed" as in "incriminate" or "entrap". On the one hand computer games are celebrations of uncertainty, on the other, this uncertainty is not real. It's just *pretend* uncertainty because computers have a problem with real randomness in so far as they can't generate randomness due to their very nature as von Neumann architecture and Turing machines. This is a key dis-tinction that separates computer games from other games. There are many forms of framed uncertainties but there is a certain edge to the notion when it comes to computer games because of their digital ontology. It almost seems as if there is a kind of longing for uncertainty, randomness and entropy in digital media that is articulated in computer games for us to explore. This kind of "double-framing" works by *showing* what is otherwise hidden. Self-reference in computer games is almost inevitable because of the density of framing problems within the medium, that is "framing the framer" (Butler 2009, 5–15)[5] in a double-bind.

The question "Is this a dream?" points to this kind of meta-con-clusion derived from the liminal state of the lucid dreamer, who is both within and outside of the dream. "He or she cannot, unless

---

5   "The frame that seeks to contain, convey, and determine what is seen (and sometimes, for a stretch, succeeds in doing precisely that) depends upon the conditions of reproducibility in order to succeed. And yet, this very reproducibility entails a constant breaking from context, a con-stant delimitation of new context, which means that the 'frame' does not quite contain what it conveys, but breaks apart every time it seeks to give definitive organization to its content. In other words, the frame does not hold anything together in one place, but itself becomes a kind of perpetual breakage, subject to a temporal logic by which it moves from place to place. As the frame constantly breaks from its context, this self-breaking becomes part of the very definition." (Butler 2009, 10)

close to waking, dream a statement referring to [that is, framing] his dream" (Bateson 1972, 191). The dynamism of ludic mediality as a phenomenon of liminality has to be described as a mode of processuality in which *suddenness* is the key element in which game and play show their specific mediality. Suddenness as an expression and symbol of the non-identical and the discontinuous in aesthetic modernity has been discussed prominently by Karl-Heinz Bohrer (1994). It is no coincidence that there are many connections to the notion of ludic mediality discussed here, because game, play and chance have been very important concepts for aesthetic modernity from Stéphane Mallarmé to surrealism to Marcel Duchamp and beyond, right up until today. It is this "dangerous" element of game and play that defines its allure.

It is because of this that the mediation of paradoxes as the core element of ludic mediality only shows itself momentarily. Alice's uncertainty and hesitation are just as brief as those of the player fighting Psycho Mantis in *Metal Gear Solid*. Shortly after these moments, the epistemic and logical borderlines between reality and fiction, actuality and virtuality, become stable again. Likewise, the experience of lucid dreaming is just a matter of seconds between dreaming and awakening.

Bateson uses the analogy of the dream because it is his goal to describe game and play as a state of liminality that "mediates" between primary and secondary processes, realising their full transgressive potential in the process. At this point a connection between different categories is established that are, however, never fully compatible. "The message 'This is play' thus sets a frame of the sort which is likely to precipitate paradox: it is an attempt to discriminate between, or to draw a line between, categories of different logical types" (Bateson 1972, 195).

For Bateson the rule-regulated "game" is differentiated from the less restricted form of "play" by its higher level of complexity because in a game the problem of framing and the resulting paradoxes are reflected upon. In play the only rule results from

the performativity of the assertion "This is play". In a game the
logico-epistemic uncertainty is driven by the question "Is this a
game?" that is at the same time reflected upon by playing the
game. Bateson as well as Niklas Luhmann's concept of medium
and form are based on the assumption that "meaning"[6] is an
effect of the processing of paradoxes. The famous paradox of
Epimenides is a blue print for the kinds of paradoxes in question
here.

This paradox results in a double-bind, an epistemic structure
Bateson was interested in as a component of a theory of schizophrenia (his path to a theory of game and play led through
mental illness, or at least what society deems as such). For
Bateson, not being able to deal with simultaneous and contrary claims that cannot be true at the same time (according to
the law of contradiction) is the very definition of the state of
schizophrenia. A schizophrenic therefore loses his or her grip
on reality because he or she cannot decide what is "real" and
what is not, and as a result, his or her mind is stuck in a loop of
recurring (im)possibilities. In games, however, Bateson discovers
a dynamic, a process that while not able to eliminate the double-
bind, *deals* with it via *temporal transgression*. For Bateson, game
and play had such a profound impact on the human mind that he
was forced to conceptualise them as an evolutionary leap in the
development of communication as a whole. The processing of
paradoxes is fundamental for communication to go beyond the
mere recognition of straight sensory signals.

Only such "playful" communication is able to develop meta-com-
munications that can process double-binds and turn them into
meaning. It is not hard to see what he had in mind, because
without being able to somehow mediate between paradoxes,

6   "Meaning" (*Sinn*) has to be understood in the sense that Luhmann gave
     the notion. In the perspective of his system theory "meaning" is in itself a
     medium that allows complex psychic and social systems to generate self
     reference and complexity. "Meaning" is therefore a prerequisite for complex
     systems as a whole. See Luhmann (1987, 92–148).

we would not be able to recognise, let alone process any kind of sign-usage, beyond strict denotation. Without understanding something to be true and false at the same time, we could not understand jokes, irony, metaphors or sarcasm. This is, of course, why the idea of an ideal language had to fail and it is of course no coincidence that Bateson was heavily influenced by Wittgenstein who began with a grandiose concept of an ideal language and arrived at a theory of games.

Bateson uses the metaphor of "map and territory" to illustrate this in psychological terms using an old semiotic figure of thought.[7] Paradoxes result from a confrontation of primary and secondary processes. Games in the sense of the question "Is this a game?" transcend the boundary between these two primordial psychological forces: "In primary process, map and territory are equated; in secondary process, they can be discriminated. In play, they are both equated and discriminated" (Bateson 1972, 191). This *coincidentia oppositorum* is perceived in brief, fleeting epiphanies of the logico-epistemic uncertainties mentioned above. Within the boundaries of the game the different layers are not mediated in the sense of a potential synthesis but as temporal successions that allow for a processing of the double-bind *by means of time*.

As a side note, this idea of processing paradoxes is one of the integral parts of Niklas Luhmann's theory, that was heavily influenced by the work of Bateson and Spencer-Brown. For Luhmann (as for Deleuze) paradoxes are not something that have to be eliminated in order to make something work but, on the contrary, are one of the most basic fundamentals of psychic and social systems. Luhmann borrows the notion of "re-entry" from the mathematician George Spencer-Brown. The term refers to an operation that enables a given system to reintegrate the basic differentiation that it, in itself, is based on, and to do so by

---

7   Those connotations to the notion of "map and territory" that connect it with the history of colonialism have to be put aside in the context of this essay, since this would be a topic of its own that can't be tackled in passing.

means of self-observation. This establishes the famous "second-order" observer that, for Luhmann, is the epistemic hallmark of modernity.

This fluctuating dynamism is what ludic mediality is about, because the temporal processing is never linear but recursive. The ludic operations always tilt from one layer into the other, so that fixed moments "before" and "after" are established: paradoxes don't get dissolved but stay in place while at the same time being processed without resulting in a stable synthesis. Ludic mediality always stays discrete, generating "meaning" as a result of the continuous processing of epistemic, logic and even ontological layers. Pathological modes of this dynamism (like schizophrenia) emerge at the exact moment when the psychic (or social) system is not able to walk this tightrope of ludic mediality anymore, when the paradoxes cannot be processed.

Before any categorisation into genres like *first-person shooters* or *adventure,* it can be said that one of the constitutive fundamentals of many computer games and their ludic mediality is a specific kind of self-reference, if not always as obvious as in *Metal Gear Solid*. It seems to be such a defining feature of many computer games that there is a clash or conflict between sophisticated techniques of immersion that try to establish "realistic"[8] game worlds and inevitable moments of self-reference that point to the artificiality, the "non-reality", of the game space. This struggle between conflicting aspects – which would be more precisely captured by the Heideggerian notion of *Streit* (strife), something I can't get into here – is constitutive of a tension that is typical for computer games. On the one hand contemporary, big budget computer games still aim at hyper realistic graphics and immersive gameplay experiences that ideally make the player forget the artificiality of the game environment, on the other

8   "Realism" in this case doesn't necessarily refer to a kind of photorealistic simulation of reality but more to the creation of believable, virtual objects. See for this distinction Esposito (1978, 270).

hand games mustn't be too realistic in order to function. The delicate balance of ludic mediality is always maintained, "total immersion", meaning a complete perceptual illusion, is nothing but a phantasm of design theory. There is always a simultaneous closeness and distance to the world of the game because a game can only work because of this distance, while at the same time it has to be immersive enough to be believable. Accordingly, Steven Poole (2000, 77) wrote in his famous book *Trigger Happy*:

> Counter-intuitively, it seems for the moment that the perfect videogame 'feel' requires the ever-increasing imaginative and physical involvement of the Player to stop somewhere short of full bodily immersion. After all, a sense of pleasurable control implies some modicum of *separation*: you are apart from what you are controlling.

It is important to note that this simultaneousness of external observation and intrinsic participation reveals one of the most distinctive characteristics of computer games, a characteristic that gets overlooked as soon as one of the perspectives is privileged. It is because of this that Sybille Krämer insists upon the observation that this simultaneousness of perceptual and epistemic layers is a mode of perception unique to cyberspaces; a hypothesis aimed at a common rhetoric critical or media and the "dissolution of the real", which I briefly mentioned earlier, when I referred to Baudrillard and Virillo:

> Against the dogmatisation of just one perspective it has to be stressed that simulations of virtual realities presuppose that there is a difference between the space that a real body occupies and the virtual space of interaction. Cyberspace depends upon the difference between virtual reality and corporality in the outside world (Krämer 1998, 36; translation by the author).

It is no wonder that this fundamental difference is emphasised in computer games in ubiquitous instances of self-reference. One example is the save-function that is, of course, a characteristic

of digital media as a whole. Through saving, the player is able
to start where he or she left off without having to start all over
again. In many instances this save-function is not only triggered
by discrete keyboard commands but is represented inside the
diegetic world of the game. The ways in which these "save-
points" are represented in game are manifold and most of the
time game designers try to integrate their appearances into the
representational logic or design of the game in an attempt to
preserve the immersion (which is unavoidable because using
a save-point is in itself a meta-action that points beyond the
diegetic world of the game). These save-points, which can take
many forms – strange objects, books, typewriters or even sofas
where the protagonist can sit down and relax – are conspicuous
in the game world. They point to the artificiality of the game by
not quite fitting "in the picture". This is why such save-points have
practically vanished. In the days of automatic, discrete saving
or server client check-ups, save-points like those described are
about to become a thing of the past.

A different and quite popular form of self-referential deixis can
be found in the use of *MacGuffins*: virtual objects with the sole
purpose of being semiotic "blank spaces" in a pan-semiotic world
where normally everything is semantically connected to "make
sense" for the player. In *Final Fantasy VII (1997)*, the player can find
certain objects that, when inspected closely, reveal themselves
to be miniature versions of the characters the player is interacting with during the game. These little figurines are virtual
objects "without meaning" because they are useless, that is,
they are meaningless in regards to actual gameplay mechanics.
They are just there, poking out of the virtual environment like a
sore thumb. They can't be used to fight, they are not part of any
kind of puzzle or quest, they are just empty signifiers that point
beyond themselves to a world outside of the game. Only the
player can recognise their meaninglessness as such by aimlessly
searching for the missing signified in a kind of parody of Derrida's
infinite semiosis.

It has to be noted though that these kinds of "useless objects" have been tamed somewhat in recent years due to what can be called a "re-labourisation" of gaming. Since the introduction of platform "achievement systems" by *Microsoft's Xbox LIVE* environment, computer games are littered with collectibles or little tasks that are unconnected to the game but that reward the player with completion tokens like trophies, badges or medals and give the tasks with a shallow sense of meaning. These meta-systems emphasise how little computer games (or shall we say most gamers?) can tolerate empty signifiers, how even the last anarchic traces of uncertainty must be tamed in order to satisfy our desire for meaning.

In a rundown part of a futuristic city in the classic PC role playing game (RPG), *Anachronox* (2001), the player encounters a non-player character (NPC) whose sole purpose is to yell in the style of crazy apocalyptic visionaries and remind all passerby NPCs of their own digital artificiality. ("You are all not real! We exist within a computer game! Look, you are constantly uttering the same few sentences! You are all not real! We exist inside a computer game".) Since those early days, references to onto-epistemic uncertainty are part of many computer games such as in the sophisticated narratives of the *Metal Gear Solid series*, *Planescape Torment* (1999), *Deus Ex* (2000) to name just a few examples, not to mention more recent games like *Portal* (2007) and *Braid* (2008) that put self-reference at the core of their design concepts.

In conclusion it can be established that games as a medium provide a certain kind of experience by allowing the simultaneous coexistence of otherwise incompatible layers, and this dynamic is amplified in computer games because of their medial foundations in digital media. Computer games, understood as a specific mode of the medium "game", highlight this dynamic as the coexistence of closeness and distance, intrinsic actor and external observer. The resulting tension is the medium in which computer games are specific actualisations. In these actualisations, the paradoxical condition of their mediality is often shown in stagings of self-reference that computer game designers tend to gravitate to, perhaps not without reason. But these paradoxical dynamics are only mirroring the human condition – the experience of being external observer and "embedded" participant, subject *and* object, at the same time, as phenomenology has told us from Husserl to Merleau-Ponty. This conflict can be experienced acutely in virtual environments and, of course, in computer games.

Computer games are the most widely distributed form of virtual reality and, as interactive media, allow an actual integration of the perspective of the participant into the perspective of the observer and because of this, both an internal and external perspective of the interacting subject. This subject therefore is at the same time distant observer and involved actor. This involvement however gets aesthetically sublimated because the dangers of being "involved" get suspended like in lucid dreams.

A few closing remarks.

When I started working in game studies at the beginning of this century, the notion of *gamification* wouldn't have been understood as it is today. At that time *gamification* would have meant the dissolution of the real in favour of a postmodern "anything goes" conception of reality (as described earlier), perhaps synonymous with a term like "aesthetisation". Although computer games already became a very large industry during the early twenty-first century, nobody would have been able to foresee the extent of pervasive gaming today. In the age of big data, geo-tagging and self-optimisation through "achievements" and "rankings", game studies needs to consider a broader notion of what game-related fields of research may be, and that is exactly what is being done at the moment. In the past we loved to pose ontological questions, and for a long time game studies was expected to deliver definitions and thereby answer the questions "What is a game and what is its nature?", But, at least for me, the more interesting way to approach this is to observe what kind of questions occur when we think about games? Because, obviously, thinking about the diversity of play is not just about different cultures and approaches to gaming but also about conceiving of ludic principles as a catalyst and prerequisite for thinking, feeling, understanding, creating understand worlds. The ubiquity of *gamification* (the application of game mechanics in non-game contexts), for example, allows us to differentiate at least three distinct layers that, in combination, constitute "games" as a specific mode of world apprehension.

1. Self-optimisation
2. Risk management
3. Mediation of paradoxes

All of these elements can be utilised to enhance the human condition ethically and aesthetically, as Kant, Schiller and Huizinga have argued, but at the same time they are used in the "games" of global capitalism where all of our lives are "at stake". For Schiller, self-optimisation would have taken the form of a pedagogical system of playful education. In today's work environments elements of gaming are often used as superficial gratification-systems that mimic playful competition in order to make us work or consume more efficiently. Risk management is the only aspect of games that is relevant to the *mathematical* theory of games, which in turn is the basis for the market-predicting algorithms that global markets are based on. Standard & Poor's, and other rating agencies, do nothing else but "play games" *with our future* and that is indeed a core ingredient of gaming itself.

Games are all about predicting the future regardless of whether this future is immediate or a hundred years from now. Uncertainty is both at the core of what is fun about games, and the reason why mathematical game theory dominates economic theory today. It's all about living with contingency. The mediation of paradoxes seems to be the last remaining space of human freedom and the place where the arts, at last, come into their own. But this is just one side of the story. Making connections perceivable that would otherwise be unperceivable and risking loss or the destruction of known boundaries are indispensable for games to work. By letting markets collapse and deliberately "raising the stakes" in the process, profits are maximised and wars are won. In an effort to conceptualise a truly interdisciplinary approach to game studies that would bring all these aspects of gaming into the equation, we have to consider the notion that games are intrinsically humanist as a romantic one.

We have to decide how to approach games as one of the great cultural resources of humanity. Gaming and playing don't mean passively embracing indifference. On the contrary, they are an active encounter with difference, and computer games, being digital media, especially allow us to practice navigating uncertainty. Historically, game studies and its subject, what I called ludic epistemology, are heirs to postmodernity in that they don't play well with intellectual laziness and superficial relativism and especially not with essentialisms. Playing games is a way to be in contact with the world in a way that doesn't allow for quick answers and handy definitions. It might be a mad world out there, but the dance of paradoxes is not just something to be feared, but something to be explored, and games as framed uncertainties allow just that.

Bibliography

Bateson, Gregory. 1972. "A Theory of Game and Fantasy" In *Steps to an Ecology of the Mind*. Northvale, NJ, London: Jason Aronson.

Bohrer, Karl-Heinz. 1994. *Suddenness: On the Moment of Aesthetic Appearance* New York: Columbia University Press.

Butler, Judith. 2009. *Frames of War: When is Life Grievable?* London, New York: Verso.

Carroll, Lewis. 1912. *Alice's Adventures in Wonderland & Through the Looking Glass*. London: Chancellor Press.

Costikyan, Greg. 2013. *Uncertainty in Games*. Cambridge, MA: MIT Press.

Dawkins, Richard. 2006. *The God Delusions*. Boston: Houghton Mifflin.

Deleuze, Gilles. 1998. *Logik des Sinns*. Frankfurt/M: Suhrkamp.

Esposito, Elena. 1998. "Fiktion und Virtualität". In *Medien – Computer – Realität*, edited by Sybille Krämer, 269–96. Frankfurt/M: Suhrkamp.

Hitchens, Christopher. 2007. *God is Not Great: How Religion Poisons Everything*. Boston, New York: Twelve.

106   Krämer, Sybille. 1998. *"Zentralperspektive – Kalkül – Virtuelle Realität. Sieben Thesen über die Weltimplikationen symbolischer Formen".* In *Medien – Welten – Wirklichkeit*, edited by G. Vattimo and W. Welsch, 27–37. München: Fink.

Lacan, Jacques. 1972. In *Jacques Lacan parle*, directed by Françoise Wolf. Brooklyn: Icarus Films. DVD.

Luhman, Niklas. 1987. *Soziale Systeme: Grundriß einer allgemeinen Theorie*, Frankfurt/M: Suhrkamp.

Ratzinger, Joseph. 2004. "Auf der Suche nach dem Frieden: Gegen erkrankte Vernunft und mißbrauchte Religion". In: *Frankfurter Allgemeine Zeitung*, June 11, 39.

Rautzenberg, Markus. 2002. *Spiegelwelt: Elemente einer Aisthetik des Bildschirmspiels*. Berlin: Logos.

Poole, Steven. 2000. *Trigger Happy: The Inner Life of Videogames*. London: 4th Estate.

Ludography

Anachronox (2001). Ion Storm. Eidos.

Bloodborne (2015). From Software. SCE Japan Studio.

Braid (2008). Number One, Inc.

Castlevania (1986). Konami.

Demons Souls (2009). From Software. SCE Japan Studio.

Deus Ex (2000). Ion Storm/Eidos Montreal. Eidos Interactive/Square Enix.

Eternal Darkness (2002). Silicon Knights. Nintendo.

Final Fantasy VII (1997). Square.

Heavy Rain (2010). Quantic Dream. Sony Computer Entertainment.

Life is Strange (2015). Dontnod Entertainment. Square Enix.

Manhunt (2003). Rockstar North. Rockstar Games.

Metal Gear Solid (1998). Konami.

Papa y Yo (2012). Vander Caballero. Minority.

Planescape Torment (1999). Black Isle Studios. Interplay Entertainment.

Portal (2007). Valve Corporation. Microsoft Game StudiosP

Psychonauts (2005). Double Fine Productions. Majesco Entertainment.

Sanitarium (1998). DreamFurge Intertainment. ASC Games.

Silent Hill (1999). Konami Computer Entertainment.

Solid Snake (1987). Hideo Kojima.

The Suffering (2004). Surreal Software. Midway Home Entertainment. Midway Games.

World of Warcraft (2004). Blizzard Entertainment.

Authors

Astrid Ensslin joined Bangor University in 2007 after receiving her PhD (summa cum laude) on electronic literature (hypertext, hypermedia and canonicity) from Heidelberg University. She has previously held Economic and Social Research Council and British Academy funded research and teaching positions at the universities of Leeds and Manchester. Her main interests are in the field of digital humanities, in particular digital culture and communication. Her current research revolves around reading digital fiction (Arts and Humanities Research Council funded) and literary gaming. Further interests include the language of videogames and gaming, language ideologies in (new) media, and studying learner language using corpus-based discourse analysis. She convenes Bangor University's Digital Economies Cluster and is Principal Investigator of the *Journal of Gaming and Virtual Worlds*.

Mathias Fuchs is an artist, musician and media critic, currently working at Leuphana University in Lüneburg. He pioneered the field of the artistic use of games and is a leading theoretician on game art and game studies. His game art and media art installations have been shown at ISEA94 and ISEA2004, resfest, ars electronica, PSi #11, futuresonic, EAST, and the Greenwich Millennium Dome. He has designed creative games for museums, urban planning and theatre performances. He is Professor at the Centre for Digital Cultures, directing the Art & Civic Media lab, which has a research focus on ludic interfaces, affective gaming and gamification. Mathias has co-edited *Rethinking Gamification*, published by meson press in 2013. He is also co-editor of the journal *Digital Culture & Society*.

Tanya Krzywinska started playing computer-based games on *Usenet* when working at Digital Equipment Corporation while doing her Masters in film. Several years later, after completing her PhD, she gave her earliest paper on horror games at one of the first ever academic conferences on games in 2000 and co-edited the first collection of essays to be devoted to the study of the relationship between games and cinema. Tanya has focused her attention mainly on games, with a particular interest in their formal properties, graphical styles and "world creation". She is Director of the Games Academy and Professor of Digital Games at Falmouth University, as well as Editor of the journal *Games and Culture* and Creative Director of *Round Table Game Studios*. At Falmouth University, Tanya has developed the Digital Games Academy, which offers a suite of games-related BA and BSc (Hons) courses in digital game art, animation, design, music, programming and writing.

Karen Palmer is a filmmaker, artist and designer of neurogames. Karen explores new formats and aesthetic production technologies with her group, Interactive Films. She fuses film, gaming, technology, wellbeing and sport. Karen's work has received international exposure and critical acclaim, including screenings at the Institute of Contemporary Arts and the British Academy of Film and Television Arts. She has exhibited at the V&A as part of the Digital Design Weekend (September 2014). She was also an invited speaker at the International WOW Talks series at Regent Street Apple Store as part of V&A events in conjunction with the London Design Festival. She is currently working on the development of a new piece entitled *FUTURESELF*.

Markus Rautzenberg is a German philosopher currently working at Freie Universität Berlin. In 2007 he received his doctoral grade in philosophy with a thesis on a theory of perturbation. Fellowships he has received include a German Research Foundation

(DFG) Doctoral Scholarship at the graduate school working with the Körper-Inszenierungen (The Staging of the Body) Research Group and a DFG Postdoctoral Fellowship at the international graduate school, working with the Interart Research Group. Since 2009, he has been a member of the research staff at the Institute for Philosophy at Freie Universität Berlin, and since 2011 heads his own DFG research project on non-visual aspects of iconicity. His main fields of research are media theory, picture theory, aesthetics, the relation of iconicity and knowledge, epistemology and game studies.

www.ingramcontent.com/pod-product-compliance
Lightning Source LLC
La Vergne TN
LVHW092339060326
832902LV00008B/721